ADVANCE PRAISE FOR
The Goddess is in the Details

The Goddess is in the Details is a champion of common sense. Advanced Witches can focus on the small and big stuff concerning the witchy lifestyle. What I enjoyed best were the incantations: fresh verses, good rhymes.

Z. Budapest, author of *The Holy Book of Women's Mysteries* and *Summoning the Fates*

Another Witch once told me what sets us apart from others is our capability to see the magickal in the mundane. Deborah Blake has created a practical method of weaving the spiritual into the daily chores of the mundane world in which we must live. Easy to read and easy to implement, *The Goddess is in the Details* is a reference and a comfort for any Witch seeking new practices to bring Pagan spirituality into every part of our lives.

Edain McCoy, author of *Advanced Witchcraft*, *The Witch's Coven*, and *If You Want to Be a Witch*

Getting back to our roots (pun intended!) and practicing our creed every day is the goal of *The Goddess is in the Details*. Fun to read and chock-full of sensible advice, Deborah Blake's new book should find a place in every Pagan's library. Whether you are a beginning Pagan just finding your way or an experienced elder in the tradition, you will find something of comfort, enjoyment, and practicality in this book. With its warm and intimate tone, it inspires the reader and reminds us that our hearts and our hearths are the abodes of our deities: our gods and goddesses are always with us.

Denise Dumars, author of *Be Blessed: Daily Devotions for Busy Wiccans and Pagans*

wisdom for
the everyday witch

John Mazarak

About the Author

Deborah Blake is a Wiccan high priestess who has been leading an Eclectic group, Blue Moon Circle, since Beltane 2004. She is the author of *Circle, Coven & Grove: A Year of Magickal Practice* (Llewellyn, 2007) and *Everyday Witch A to Z* (Llewellyn, 2008), and she has written a number of articles for Pagan publications, including *Llewellyn's 2008 Witches' Companion.*

Deborah was also a finalist in the Pagan Fiction Award Contest, and her short story, "Dead and (Mostly) Gone," is included in *The Pagan Anthology of Short Fiction: 13 Prize Winning Tales* (Llewellyn, 2008). She is currently working on her fourth book for Llewellyn, as well as a novel featuring, naturally, a Witch.

When not writing, Deborah manages the Artisans' Guild, a cooperative shop she founded with a friend in 1999, and works as a jewelry maker, tarot reader, ordained minister, and intuitive energy healer. She lives in a 100-year-old farmhouse in rural upstate New York with five cats who supervise all her activities, both magickal and mundane.

Deborah Blake

The Goddess
is in the
Details

wisdom for
the everyday witch

Llewellyn Publications
WOODBURY, MINNESOTA

FIRST EDITION
First Printing, 2009

Book design by Rebecca Zins
Cover design by Ellen R. Dahl
Cover and part page illustration by Fiona King

Llewellyn is a registered trademark of Llewellyn Worldwide, Ltd.

Library of Congress Cataloging-in-Publication Data
Blake, Deborah, 1960-
The goddess is in the details: wisdom for the everyday witch / Deborah Blake.—1st ed.
  p. cm.
Includes bibliographical references.
ISBN 978-0-7387-1486-8
1. Wiccans. 2. Witches. 3. Neopagans. 4. Goddess religion. I. Title.
BP605.W53B53 2009
299′.94—dc22

2008056152

Llewellyn Worldwide does not participate in, endorse, or have any authority or responsibility concerning private business transactions between our authors and the public.

All mail addressed to the author is forwarded but the publisher cannot, unless specifically instructed by the author, give out an address or phone number.

Any Internet references contained in this work are current at publication time, but the publisher cannot guarantee that a specific location will continue to be maintained. Please refer to the publisher's website for links to authors' websites and other sources.

Llewellyn Publications
A Division of Llewellyn Worldwide, Ltd.
2143 Wooddale Drive, Dept. 978-0-7387-1486-8
Woodbury, MN 55125-2989
www.llewellyn.com

Printed in the United States of America

CONTENTS

PART THREE:
The Outer Witch

PART FOUR:
The Social Witch

CONTENTS

DEDICATION

As always, to the women of Blue Moon Circle: you are the earth that supports me, the air that I breathe, the water that sustains me, and the fire that lights my way. Without you, my life would be a poorer place (and these books would be much shorter).

And many thanks to my "borrowed" husbands for all the assists with fences, lamps, garden beds, and the rest. I hope that someday I will find a guy of my own who is as great as all of you. In the meantime, if you could just come over for an hour next Saturday…

To my family, who accept me as I am no matter how strange a road I walk. And especially the two who have chosen to walk the path a little ways with me—Jenn and Addy. I could think of no one with whom I would rather share the journey.

To the world's best editors: Elysia Gallo and Rebecca Zins. Thanks for always making me look good and for being such a pleasure to work with. You are truly a gift from the gods.

And most of all, to my readers. There is no greater satisfaction for a writer than to have someone say, "I read your book and I really loved it." Thanks to all those who have reached out to tell me how much my work has touched their lives, to those who have recommended my books to others, and to all those Witches who kindly said, "I can't wait to read the next one."

Here it is. Many bright blessings to you all.

There are many books out there for the Witch who is just starting out. Lovingly (or not so lovingly) referred to by many of us as "Wicca 101" books, they instruct those who are new to the Craft in the basics of magickal practice, which tools to use, and how to cast spells.

This is not one of those books.

Sorry.

That is not to say that this book won't be of some use to you if you are a beginning Witch. It is my hope that the topics I cover within these pages will help all those who follow the Old Ways, whether they have been practicing for a month or for twenty years.

But in truth, this book was written primarily with more experienced Witches in mind. There are a few places where I cover the basics, of course, primarily as a refresher or to make sure that we are all on the same page. But if you need to know how to pronounce "athame" or perform a simple quarter call, you need a different book.

So, you might ask, who *is* this book for?

It is for any Witch who has mastered the fundamentals and longs to go deeper. It is for the Pagan who has been on his or her path for a while and feels like something is missing…but doesn't quite know what. And it is for anyone who believes that being a Witch is less about what color candle you light than about how you live your life every day.

Some of us may reach this point after a few weeks of practice; for others, it may take years. But if you are searching for ways to integrate your spiritual beliefs as a Pagan with your everyday life, then this book is for you.

The book has six parts, each covering various aspects of the Witch's life. I suggest that you read the first part—well, first. It covers some of the elements that I will refer to throughout the book. Other than that, though, feel free to go to whichever part suits your fancy, catches your eye, or meets your needs at the moment. Or read through them all in order, it's up to you.

I have tried to answer many of the questions that have come up in my own life or that have been brought to me in my role as high priestess. Questions like "How does being a Witch help you deal with a crisis?" "How do I share my space with non-Pagans?" Or even "How can I have an altar if I am still in the broom closet?"

In every chapter, I address the issues that confront us as we live our lives as Pagans in a non-Pagan world. I answer some questions and raise a few more in the process, because part of my intention here is to get us all thinking and talking about what it is that makes us Witches and how we can bring that part of us more fully into our everyday existence.

At the end of each chapter, there are small, optional extras: some are called "something to think about" and others are called "something to try." I hope that they will amuse, assist, and encourage you as you travel your path.

The Goddess is in the Details is about bringing our best witchy selves to every moment of our mundane lives…even if no one knows it but us.

I love being a Witch, and not just at full moons or on the sabbats—although I love those too. I love being a Pagan every day of the year.

Why? Because I look at the world differently than I did before I discovered I was a Witch, and that difference makes my life a better place. Being a Pagan influences every facet of my life, bringing light and laughter and a new perspective to the everyday tasks and trials we all deal with 365 days a year.

To me, being a Witch is more than worshipping the goddess under a glowing sky or celebrating Beltane with one hundred of my closest friends (some of whom I just met). It is how I make choices, mark the important moments of my life, and bring reverence and mirth to all that I do.

Being a Witch is not just the road to who I am, it is the journey itself. And how I travel on that journey makes all the difference.

So come, join me on the journey that is the well-lived Pagan life. And may the goddess send her brightest blessings to speed you on your way.

part one

the
everyday
WITCH

A Note on Names

If you are reading this book, you probably know that you are a Pagan. But Pagans go by many names—which one should you use? Truthfully, it probably doesn't matter, at least insofar as this book is concerned. Many Pagans call themselves Witches. Some of them also use the term Wiccan, a more modern invention. This book is written for them all.

Wicca itself is the name for a modern practice of Witchcraft based on the "old ways," or (insert definition here). The term *Witch* covers a vast spectrum of folks, all of whom practice magick in one way or another. *Pagan* is a more general term that covers anyone who believes in a religion that is nature-based and usually polytheistic (which is a big word for believing in more than one god, usually including a goddess).

Pagans can be found in every country in the world, and all the earliest religions in the world were Pagan in nature. In fact, the word *Pagan* originally meant "dweller in the country" and eventually came to be used for anyone who was not a Christian, since the Christian faith took hold first in the large cities with the royalty of the time and then spread outward.

What does any of this mean to the modern Witch? Really, it just means that you can call yourself whatever name you find most comfortable. I call myself a Wiccan, but I have friends who refer to themselves as Pagans or Witches and don't like to be called Wiccans. Nevertheless, we all agree on the same basic spiritual beliefs and practice together with ease.

Still, most folks want to find the name that fits their beliefs and practices best. They also don't want to be misunderstood or lumped in with others whose belief systems they don't truly share. So how do you know whether to call yourself a Pagan, a Witch, or a Wiccan?

Let's see what the experts have to say.

In his book *The Mystic Foundation: Understanding & Exploring the Magical Universe*, Christopher Penczak describes Paganism as "the revival of the pre-Christian Pagan traditions of Europe." He goes on to explain that modern Pagans (or Neopagans, as some call them, to differentiate between the old and the new) "seek to recapture the Earth-reverent, nature-oriented traditions of ages past, where nature was seen as an expression of divinity." (1)

Penczak also says that "all Witches are Pagans, but not all Pagans identify as Witches," and admits that some people consider Witchcraft and Wicca to be the same thing, while others see Wicca as a subset of Witchcraft, which in turn is a subset of Paganism.

He adds:

> Wicca is considered to be the modern revival of the religion of Witchcraft. Witchcraft is an art, science, and spiritual tradition based on Pagan traditions of the ancient world ... One school of thought views Wicca as the religion and Witchcraft as the collection of techniques. Others see Witchcraft as the more traditional practice and Wicca as the modern, eclectic form of the Craft. (2)

Confused yet?

Okay, let's see what Eileen Holland says in *The Wicca Handbook* (which, along with Christopher's, is one of my favorites):

> Modern witches follow in the tradition of our earliest ancestors and are the shamans and healers of the twenty-first century. We are the priests and priestesses of the Great Goddess; we practice the ancient art of sacred magic in a modern world. (3)

Now, you'll notice that they don't disagree with each other at all, although their emphasis is a little different. Holland focuses on the goddess and our relationship to her, whereas Penczak takes a broader view. But they both mention ancient practices and traditions, and the importance of magick as a component of the religion. (And you might have noticed that, like me, Penczak capitalizes the word Witch, and Holland doesn't. Still confused? Let's move on.)

In *The Witch's Guide to Life*, author Kala Trobe has a slightly different take on the Wiccan/Witch question. She says:

> Wicca is ethical, while Traditional Witchcraft is amoral. In Traditional Witchcraft, emphasis is placed on taking responsibility for one's actions and on intent. The forces of the Universe are seen as neutral (like weather) rather than good and evil. Curses and hexes are used for self-preservation, whereas a Wiccan would never curse, believing in the law of threefold return and the ethics of "An' it Harm None." (4)

I'm not sure that I would completely agree with this definition, although for the most part it is probably fairly accurate. Many of the Witches I know, while not considering themselves Wiccan by any means, have adopted the "harm none" rule of the Wiccan Rede and would be very hesitant to curse or hex (although admittedly these were and are tools of the traditional Witch).

Most Witches seem to believe in "what you put out comes back to you," whether or not they go along with the "times three" part of the Wiccan belief, and I think that Wiccans (and not just Witches) emphasize personal responsibility and intent.

So what are we left with? I like Kala's definition of a Witch, whether Traditional or Wiccan. She says that a Witch is:

> anybody, whether Wiccan or otherwise, who: Acts positively to enhance his or her life using magick; worships the old gods, in whatever form, even as simple energies inherent in nature; accepts responsibility for his or her own actions; follows the cycles of the seasons with magickal and practical awareness; works with lunar and stellar tides, and celebrates the full moon, however quietly; strives toward self-improvement, often involving "initiation" experiences; [and] thinks of him- or herself as a witch. (5)

This is one of the best descriptions of what a Witch is that I have seen. (And I have seen *a lot* of descriptions.) There may be a few small points that don't apply to you, but if the majority seem to fit, I believe that you can safely call yourself a Witch.

Whether or not you also call yourself a Wiccan is up to you. Some folks believe that Wiccans primarily follow the practices laid down by the early Pagans who established Wicca, such as Gerald Gardner and those who followed him. Others think it depends on whether or not you base your practice on the rule of "harm none" and believe in the threefold rule.

Personally, I was trained and instructed by a high priestess who called herself a Wiccan, so that is the name I am comfortable using. I don't particularly stick to the traditional Wiccan practices, but I do try to adhere as much as possible to the Wiccan Rede ("An it harm none, do as ye will").

In truth, what really matters is that we believe in the gods and in each other. So when I use the word Witch in this book, feel free to substitute Wiccan or Pagan if that's what feels right to you. You will see that I use Witch and Pagan more or less interchangeably, less because they have identical meanings (which they don't) than because I want to make the point that the information in this book applies to everyone. Because no matter what name we use, we are all united in our faith in the old gods and in our travels down that wonderful path that is Witchcraft.

Something to Think About:

What do you call yourself? Did you choose the title yourself, or did someone else choose it for you? What do you think that name means, and how do you think others view you because of it?

1   Penczak, The Mystic Foundation, 226.

2   Ibid., 236–237.

3   Holland, The Wicca Handbook, 5.

4   Trobe, The Witch's Guide to Life, 8.

5   Ibid., 9.

CHAPTER 1

So You're a Witch...Now What?

Going Beyond the Basics

I will never forget the night, over ten years ago now, when I discovered that I was a Witch. A friend had been inviting me to come to Pagan events at her house for a while, but I kept saying no because I wasn't the kind of person who enjoyed doing things with groups of people—especially when those groups were made up of a bunch of people I didn't know.

But one Halloween, she persuaded me to come. There would only be a small, informal gathering, she said; a feast followed by a ritual. "Really, I think you'll like it."

So I went. It turned out that when she said "only a few people," she actually meant thirty or forty. And they were all a bit odd; they dressed funny, said things like "merry meet," and many of them insisted on hugging me even though we'd never met. *Oh, dear,* I thought—I *shouldn't have come.* Not my kind of thing at all.

But the feast food was good, and the people seemed nice (if a bit bizarre), and I was already there. So I stayed. And when it got dark, we went out to the park next to her house and stood in a circle. And there, amid the trees, in a clearing lit only by moonlight and candle flame, something unexpected happened.

The circle was cast, the quarters called, the gods invoked, and I felt an indefinable *something* inside me shift and change. I could sense a connection with nature and with those people who had only moments before been strangers. And for the first time in my life, I touched the gods, and they touched me back.

Never in all my years of searching—through the Judaism I was raised in, the Unitarian Church I attended in my teens and twenties, the Buddhism I'd studied after that—never had I felt with any certainty that there was, in fact, a god. But on that Samhain night, in that circle in the park, I was suddenly absolutely sure: sure that there was deity around me and inside me, sure that what I had found was the right path for me. I was a Witch, and I had come home.

After that night, I joined my friend's Eclectic study group/circle and began my exploration of Wicca and Witchcraft. After five years of absorbing her wisdom and practicing both with the group and on my own, I followed a year and a day of advanced practice and eventually became a high priestess in my own right. Not too long after that, I founded my own group, Blue Moon Circle, with whom I still practice today.

That was my path to becoming a Witch. And in truth, it was less a matter of becoming a Witch than it was finding out that there was a name for that which I had been all along.

Every Witch's story is different. Some seem almost to have been born to the Craft, either through heredity or inclination. Others stumble upon it during college, or like me come to it almost unexpectedly later in life after trying and rejecting many other paths.

But as different as the roads to becoming a Witch seem to be, most of us have much in common.

For instance, that feeling of having finally come home is something that you hear about over and over. The excitement at discovering that there is a name for who and what you are. The joy when you meet someone else who shares your beliefs.

And most of us spend our first few years in more or less the same way. We buy a book or two (or ten, or a hundred) and try to learn all we can. We memorize correspondences for herbs and stones, planets and candle colors. And we practice magick: magick for prosperity (which often works) and for love (which often doesn't). And alone or together, we stand under the full moon and gaze upon the face of the goddess with awe and joy in our hearts. We are Witches, and that is a wonderful thing.

But sooner or later, many of us come to a time in our practice when that is no longer enough. There are only so many correspondences, after all, and once you are more experienced with magickal work, they often are not even needed. (Although they don't hurt, either.)

The glory of the Lady in the night sky and the majesty of the Horned God's stag still have the power to move us, but it has begun to seem, perhaps, that something is missing. And maybe we have met one or two of those truly magickal people who seem to have attained a level of witchy existence that still hovers just beyond our reach, no matter how many books we've read or how much we have practiced our Craft.

So what do they know that we don't, and how do we take that next step along the path that is Witchcraft?

I believe the answer is simple: become an Everyday Witch. Instead of just practicing your Craft on new moons, full moons, and eight sabbats a year, be a Witch all day, every day. In short, find as many ways as possible to integrate your spiritual beliefs as a Pagan into your mundane life.

The Witches we meet that seem to have that "extra something" are the ones who truly walk their talk, day in and day out. They don't know any special secrets passed down from generation to generation. They aren't smarter or more dedicated than the rest of us. They have simply taken the next step along the path. And should you so choose, you can take it too.

Something to Try:
Find one example of a Witch you respect, either personally or through his or her writing, and pick some facet of what he or she does that you can adopt into your own life.

The Seven Beliefs at the Heart of Being a Witch

Being Pagan is as much a way of life as it is a religion. The purpose of this book is to help you find ways to integrate your spiritual beliefs into your everyday life. But each Witch is an individual with a very particular take on what it means to be Pagan. So how is it possible to write a book that works for everyone who reads it?

Well, it's not, really. Perhaps there will be bits and pieces that you feel don't apply to your particular situation or view of the world. But by and large, no matter who we are and how we see ourselves, there are some beliefs that are shared by most Witches and that shape the way we live our lives. These beliefs form the basis for our practice as Witches and make the way we look at the universe different from those who are not Pagan.

The Wiccan Rede: An It Harm None, Do As Ye Will

Whether or not they call themselves Wiccans, most Witches follow the rule known as the Wiccan Rede: "Eight words the Wiccan Rede fulfill, an it harm none, do as ye will."

This rule seems fairly simple: as long as what you do doesn't hurt anyone, you can do whatever you want. Of course, if you have been practicing

Witchcraft for longer than a week or two, you will probably have figured out that the Wiccan Rede is anything but simple.

For one thing, it is impossible to predict whether any given action will eventually have a negative effect somewhere down the line. No matter how well intentioned, it is always possible that something you do will accidentally hurt someone else.

In addition, there is the complication that when we say "harm none," we also mean ourselves. In theory, this means that anyone following the Wiccan Rede would never do anything that would harm him- or herself. That's right, put down those French fries.

Okay, so we all agree that it is impossible to follow the Wiccan Rede to the letter twenty-four hours a day, seven days a week, and never in any way cause harm to ourselves or another human being. So where does that leave us? Do we throw out this rule entirely?

Of course not. As with most spiritual and religious "rules" or "laws," we use the Wiccan Rede as a guide for our intentions. We strive to attain this goal, even as we know that there are times when we may fall short. But as Witches, this rule shapes the core of our lives and how we live them.

What You Put Out Is What You Get Back: The Law of Returns

The Rule of Three, which asserts that for every action there is a threefold return, can be a source for debate in the witchy world. Some folks insist that each action is returned in equal measure, not times three. But most Pagans would agree on the basic notion that what you put out into the universe is what you get back.

This is an extremely important idea and the basis for much of the rest of our Pagan beliefs. Think for a moment about what this rule means for how we live our lives. To begin with, it means that much of what happens to us (although by no means all) is in our own hands. If what we put out into the universe is positive and beneficial, then what we get back will also be mostly positive and beneficial.

It also means that we have the power to shape our own lives and to create positive changes in the world around us, which leads us to the next core Pagan belief.

Personal Responsibility: Free Will for All

Unlike many of the religions we may have grown up with, in which our lives are dictated by a stern and often angry god, Witchcraft is at heart a religion based on personal responsibility. The gods may send us trials and tribulations to help us learn and grow, but they are neither vengeful nor petty. How we deal with what the universe hands us is strictly up to us. So you've lost your job—do you sit on the couch and cry, or do you take this as an opportunity to pursue new options? If you're a Witch, you probably do a spell to ask for a great job to come your way. If you're a Witch who walks her talk, you then also go out and do your best to find that perfect position, and do everything in your power to make it happen.

The corollary to believing in personal responsibility is the belief in free will. Think about it: if you are responsible for your actions and all the things that result from those actions, then it makes sense that you cannot be responsible for other people's actions. Obviously, I'm not talking about taking care of children; that's a whole other issue. But it does mean that all capable adults are responsible for their own lives.

So Witches can and should do what they can to improve their own lives. But they cannot make decisions for other people, which means never working magick that might interfere with another person's free will. For instance, you can do a spell to bring you a good job, but you cannot ask for that job to be taken away from someone else in order that you might have it.

As Above, So Below: Words Have Power

We talked about the belief that what you put out into the universe is what you get back; Witches believe this on a very elemental level, in a way that affects every aspect of our lives. It is not just a matter of what you *do*. If you are a Pagan, what you say, what you think, and what you believe can also have a very real effect on the world around you.

Witches believe that words have power; this is one of the reasons that we recite our spells aloud. By saying the words out loud, we are announcing to the universe our intention—whether it is increasing prosperity or letting go of sorrow. We also believe that symbols can be used to heighten the effects of words and to stand for objects or ideas. For instance, we might use a single coin in a prosperity spell to symbolize the money we wish to earn.

As *above, so below* means not only that we have the power to effect change through symbolism and our connection with the universe, but also that we must be careful with our words and thoughts. For instance, if words have power, and what you put out is what you get back, think about what happens when you say, "I hate you." Right, and you thought the French fries were bad for you.

Most of us are accustomed to walking through life being fairly careless about what we say. Being a Witch, and more aware, means that we no longer have that option.

Magick Is Real, and We Can Use It to Bring about Positive Change

One of the things that sets Witches apart from most other people is our use of magick. We don't expect to be able to twitch our noses and turn people into toads (although sometimes that might be handy). But with a combination of our belief in our own ability to bring about positive change and the power of words and symbols, Witches use intent and focus to alter the world in which we live. By tapping into the universal energies that magick can connect us with, we can create a new and better reality.

Of course, with power comes responsibility and the need to use that power wisely. Most experienced Witches have learned that magick is not always the best solution to all of life's problems. Many issues in our lives can be handled in mundane ways, and there are certain situations in which magickal interference is probably a bad idea (messing with the weather, for instance, almost always backfires).

On the other hand, magick can be a truly useful tool in dealing with many of the ups and downs of everyday life if it is used carefully and with integrity. As long as we remember that what we put out is what we will get back, as well as the rules of personal responsibility and free will, the practice of magick can be an important facet of the everyday life of a Witch.

We Are a Part of Nature

All Pagans, whether Witches or not, have at least one thing in common: we respect nature and believe that we are a part of it, rather than above it. Traditional religious doctrines, like those found in Christianity, often view humans as being somehow superior to nature. Pagans, on the other hand, see ourselves more as guardians than as owners.

Witchcraft is often referred to as a nature-based religion. Witches follow the natural cycles of the world around us, from the waxing and waning of the moon to the eternal Wheel of the Year. We strive to connect with nature, whether stone or herb, bird or beast. Our gods are the wild, primordial forces of old, and we call upon the power of earth, air, fire, and water in our rituals.

So is it possible to be a Witch without having that special connection to nature? Most of us would say no. We don't all have to plant gardens or live in the country, but we do all need to find ways in which to nurture, appreciate, and interact with the natural world that surrounds us. How we do this is different for every Witch, but connecting to nature, and through nature to the gods and to ourselves, is at the heart of being a Pagan and a Witch.

The Divine Is in Everything, Including Us

To be a Witch is to be divine—or at least to have some element of the divine within. Pagans believe in the old gods; for most of us, that means both a goddess and a god, or at least some abstract version of deity. But we also believe that there is an element of the divine in everything: a little piece of deity in every blade of grass, every tree, and in every creature who flies, swims, crawls, or walks—including us. Some part of that which is greater than we are is also a part of us and so makes us great.

This may seem like a difficult concept to grasp, but it is at the heart of what it means to be a Witch. This connection to the universe and to the divine gives us both power and responsibility. It also connects us to every other living being. And because we are not separate from deity, we can each talk to our gods without needing the intercession of a priest or any other authority figure.

In truth, all Witches are priests and priestesses in their own right. Each of us can speak to the gods and know we are heard. There is no separation between deity and worshiper. Neither is there a separation between the magick and the mundane; the divine exists in the midst of everyday life because that is where we live.

In the chapters that follow, we will look at the many ways that these seven core beliefs influence us as Witches and as human beings. And it is my hope that as we walk this path together, we will all find new and rewarding ways to integrate our spiritual beliefs into our everyday lives.

Something to Think About/Something to Try:

Take a look at these seven core beliefs. Try to think of at least one way in which each one shapes your actions or the way you look at the world. If you belong to a group or have other friends who are Witches, you can each make a list and compare them to see which things are the same and which are different.

The Power of Words and Belief

How to Bring About Positive Change

Remember that childhood saying, "Sticks and stones can break my bones, but words will never hurt me"? Well, don't bet on it. In fact, words can hurt a great deal, as anyone who has repeatedly been labeled with a nasty name (like "fat," or "stupid," or "useless") can tell you.

But words can also help you, if you use them wisely and with positive intent. Witches use words in this way when they cast spells, of course, but this is only one manner in which these powerful tools can be utilized to create positive change in our lives.

The Power of Words and the External World

We've already talked a little bit about the importance of the concept of the law of returns: what you put out is what you get back. At its most basic level, the effect this can have on your life is obvious—if you walk around saying negative things about others, in all probability others will end up saying negative things about you.

But hopefully, most of us are not that kind of person. And while it would certainly benefit all of us to be more careful about how often we say something derogatory about someone else, that hardly seems like a life-changing use of words.

What *can* be life-changing, however, is to look at our overall use of words and what we are putting out into the universe.

If you stop and listen to yourself, you will probably be amazed by how often you say something negative. This doesn't mean you're a bad person; we all do it, mostly without any real intent or awareness. Think about the following phrases and whether or not you've used any of them lately:

- I hate (insert name of politician, family member, or coworker here).
- I could just kill him.
- This weather sucks.
- I hate my life (or hair, body, smile, etc.).
- I have the crappiest car (or apartment, job, or relationship).
- My kid (or husband, boss, mother, etc.) is driving me crazy.
- I never have enough money (or a good relationship, or any fun).
- I feel like shit.
- Life is so unfair.
- Goddamn it.

Obviously, I could go on all day, but you get the point. Most of us (yes, me included) say things like this every day without even thinking about it. But look at all that negativity that gets put out into the world, and think about the effect of saying something like "I never have enough money" over and over and over again. If you're a Witch, and you believe that what you put out is what you get back, you've just told the universe that you will never have enough money—and guess what? You never will.

So how do we change this? Well, that is both very simple and very difficult. As we all know, it can be very hard to break ingrained habits, especially those that are primarily unconscious. The trick here is to become *more conscious*. Pay attention to what you say, and when you find yourself putting negative thoughts out into the world, intentionally substitute something positive instead.

For instance, you are talking to your best friend and you hear yourself saying "my life sucks." Don't beat yourself up (it's painful, and you'll get blood all over the furniture). Just notice what you've said and add, "but I'm sure that's changing," or "but I'm working on making it better." Initially, you will find yourself doing this a lot, but over time, you will discover that this kind of positive mindset becomes automatic, and you don't even need to think about it.

But what if your life really does suck? Well, first of all, does it really? Certainly there are people whose lives are truly horrible, but for most of us it is more likely to be a matter of not having everything we want or facing problems that seem overwhelming. And looking on the positive side not only makes those problems easier to bear, it also makes it more likely that we will find ways to create beneficial changes. Remember: what you put out is what you get back.

So try saying some of these:

- I can accomplish anything I put my mind to.
- My life is getting better every day.
- I am truly blessed.
- I may not have everything I want, but I have everything I need.

If you are at all up on popular culture, you will probably recognize these as what are often referred to as "positive affirmations." A lot of non-Pagans have begun to see the importance of using and believing in positive words. There is even a book out called *The Secret* that is based in large part on the concept of purposely putting out what you want to get back. Of course, that's no secret to us Witches, is it?

If you are looking for scientific proof to back up your spiritual belief in the power of words, check out the book *The Hidden Messages in Water* by Masaru Emoto. Emoto is a Japanese scientist who did experiments that proved that molecules of water are affected by our thoughts, words, and feelings. The book is filled with photographs showing the crystalline formations within water and how they can be altered by speaking negative or positive words such as *love* or *hate*, as well as the changes produced by music and ideas.

The Power of Words
and the Internal Monologue

Even more important than their effect on the world around us is the effect that words can have on the world inside our own heads. Oh, yeah, you *know* what I'm talkin' about. We all have that little voice in the back of our minds—the one that says, "I'm not good enough," or "I'm so ugly," or "stupid, stupid, stupid." (And we're not even going to mention the voice that says, "It won't hurt if I have just one more brownie.")

When those words get repeated over and over, they become what's called an "internal monologue." And sadly, our own internal voices often have a more harmful effect on our lives than anything that is said to us by someone else. Not only are they harder to argue with, but often they become such a part of our internal landscape that we don't notice them anymore.

So take a minute and think about what the voice in the back of your head says to you. (No, not the bit about the brownie—the other stuff.) Does it tell you not to try because you might fail? Does it tell you that no one will ever love you because you're not worth loving?

Now imagine yourself standing in front of that little voice (mine looks a bit like a crabby elf, but you can use whatever mental image works for you). Are you with me? Okay, now look that internal monologue munchkin in the eye and repeat after me: "Oh, shut up." Then say it again, louder.

There are few words in the world that have more power than the ones we use to describe ourselves or the situations in which we find ourselves as we walk the paths of our everyday lives. I believe that many of us have reclaimed the term "Witch" in part because it has so much power behind it. When I call myself a Witch, it makes me feel strong and connected.

What words do you use to describe yourself and your life? Are they positive or negative? Do you say can—or can't? Is your glass half full or half empty?

When you listen to that inner voice, pick out the words that hurt you or hold you back from following your dreams. If you want, you can write them down on a piece of paper. Then replace them with new words, words that will help instead of hurt, words that will lend you strength instead of weakening your resolve. And when you hear that voice in the back of your head (yes, you have to actually pay attention), gently correct it. If it says "I hate myself," you say "I love myself." If it says "stupid," you say "smart." And, if it makes you feel better, feel free to keep telling that crabby elf to shut up.

The trick is to do this often and with feeling. Believe it or not, you will eventually replace your old, negative internal monologue with the new, positive one. And that, my friend, is the power of words.

Words and the Witches' Rede of Chivalry

In 1984, Ed Fitch wrote a popular book called *Magical Rites from the Crystal Well*. (1) Primarily a book of rituals taken from the long-running Pagan magazine *Crystal Well*, it started with a statement he called "the Witches' Rede of Chivalry"—kind of like a Ten Commandments for Witches. Although written in the flowery and archaic style used by many Neopagans at that time, it contained within its list of twenty-one rules much that is to be admired and that still makes sense to us today.

Chivalry is a term that isn't used much these days, but essentially it means a code of honor. Just as the Knights of the Round Table were said to have followed the rules of chivalry, "the Witches' Rede of Chivalry" suggests a list of rules for Witches to heed. Among them, there are four that deal specifically with how we as Witches use our words. (You knew there had to be a point to this, right?)

- "A Witch's word must have the validity of a signed and witnessed oath. Thus, give thy word sparingly, but adhere to it like iron."
- "Refrain from speaking ill of others, for not all truths of the matter may be known."
- "Pass not unverified words about another, for hearsay is, in large part, a thing of falsehoods."
- "Be thou honest with others, and have them know that honesty is likewise expected of them." (2)

If you look at these four statements closely, you can see that they are basi-cally saying the following: be honest, let others know you expect honesty from them, don't say negative things about others, and stand behind what you say.

All these "rules" go back to our belief in the power of words. Honesty may be optional for some, but if you are a Witch who believes that what you put out is what you get back, you *really* don't want to go around lying, spreading gossip that might harm others, or breaking promises.

And I'm not just saying that you don't want to do those things because they might come back to bite you in the butt, although that's likely to be true. With the knowledge of the power that words give us comes the responsibility to use them wisely, just like any other tool at our disposal.

You wouldn't use your athame to clean your nails, would you? Or prop open your door with your Book of Shadows? So why would you intentionally misuse your words by lying or making a promise you don't intend to keep?

If you are a Witch who is serious about walking your talk, then your use of words in your everyday life has to be as carefully thought out as your use of words to practice magick. As above, so below—there is no difference between mundane life and magickal life in the big picture, and you are a Witch all day, every day, even when you are not consciously thinking about being one. So try your best to use your words accordingly.

....

Positive Magick:
Marion Weinstein's "Words of Power"

One of my favorite Pagan books is Marion Weinstein's classic *Positive Magic: Occult Self-Help*. (3) In it, Ms. Weinstein explores many of the deeper issues and ideas behind modern Witchcraft, including the importance of words. In her chapter entitled"Words of Power, The Work of Self-Transformation," she says:

> Words are symbols. They represent ideas, which are invisible; yet words themselves can be written on a page, or otherwise perceived tangibly by our immediate senses. Even unsighted people can use words via hearing, or by the use of Braille. Deaf people can use a sign language or think the words. Anyone accustomed to working with his/her imme-diate senses can build a bridge to the Invisible Realm by way of words;

they help us span both Worlds. Words are tools; they work in invisible ways to create visible results. (4)

When she talks about the Invisible Realm, she is referring to the theory that there are two worlds: the world that we perceive as we walk through it and the invisible world that lies all around us. Both these worlds coexist, and what we do in the visible realm can affect what happens in the powerful invisible realm, although we can see only the effects in the more concrete physical one.

Which brings us back to the power of words to bring about change. One of the best examples of a practical application of this theory is Weinstein's "Words of Power." I have used this technique myself and found it very helpful. I recommend that if you haven't yet read her book, you should run, not walk, to the nearest bookstore to buy a copy. For now, I will give you the basics.

Essentially, Words of Power uses a series of ideas based on some of the basic principles of Witchcraft. You create a statement—your Words of Power—in which you specify your goal. Then you recite these words with the intent of moving this positive energy from the visible world into the invisible world and thus creating the desired change. Generally, you would recite your Words of Power regularly; for instance, every night for a month or until you achieved your goal.

This may sound complicated, but in truth it is quite simple. Look at the example that Weinstein uses for the goal of fulfillment:

1. There is One Power
2. And this Power is *perfect fulfillment.*
3. And I, (your name here), am a perfect manifestation of this Power.
4. Therefore, *perfect fulfillment* is mine, here and now.
5. For the good of all,
6. And according to free will,
7. And so it must be. (5)

This statement acknowledges that we are all part of deity (the gods are in us as well as around us) and therefore capable of effecting change. It also is spoken in the present tense to represent the belief that, on some level, the change is already taking place.

One of my favorite aspects of the Words of Power is the inclusion of statements five and six: *for the good of all and according to free will.* By adding these phrases, you can avoid unintentionally doing magickal work that has a negative result or interferes with someone else's free will. In fact, it can't hurt to add this at the end of any spell you do, just in case.

The Power of Words and Spellcasting

Of course, no discussion of Witches and words would be complete without talking about magick and spellcasting. After all, what's the fun in being a Witch if you can't work a bit of magick now and then?

It's important to remember that being a Witch doesn't begin and end with magickal work. In fact, magick and spells are a fairly small part of being an Everyday Witch. Let's face it, most of us spend more time doing the dishes than we spend casting spells. (If only we could come up with a spell to do the dishes for us—now *that* would be power!)

On the other hand, spells can be an important tool in bringing about positive change in our lives; knowing that is part of what makes us Witches. So what is the best way to use magick to improve our lives?

First, save it for the important stuff. You don't use a power drill to tighten the loose screw in your wobbly chair, you use a screwdriver. In the same way, you don't need to cast a spell to have a nice day or cook a good meal. On the other hand, if you are cooking dinner for your picky mother-in-law for the first time, it might be helpful to do a little spell to ask for help in making things go well.

Second, don't forget to do your part. We can't expect magick to do everything for us; remember, the goddess helps those who help themselves. So you can do the spell for help in the kitchen, but you'll also want to pick up a few cookbooks, practice the meal ahead of time, and put out the good china. Magickal work is all about increasing our own potential, and the more effort we put into it, the more likely it is to work.

Third, focus on the positive and believe in yourself. Even when the obstacles seem overwhelming (the woman cried at your wedding, but they weren't tears of joy), it is important to have faith that your magick will work. Do the prep work, cast your spell, then just move forward assuming it will all turn out fine.

Last but equally important, choose your words carefully. If you are using a spell that someone else wrote (and there is nothing wrong with that), check it over carefully to make sure that it says what you want it to say. Better yet, write the spell yourself and put all the energy of your wish for success into it as you put the words onto paper. But remember to avoid anything that will interfere with free will. For instance, in this case you could do a spell to make your food taste wonderful and the evening go smoothly, but you shouldn't do a spell to make your mother-in-law love you, no matter what. (And no, you can't do a spell to turn her into a toad, either. Sorry about that.)

Spellcasting is probably the best example of the power of words, and as with the other uses of words that we talked about, we must all remember to use that power responsibly, never in a frivolous or malicious manner.

When used with positive intent and backed by the force of your will, spells can be a potent tool for creating beneficial changes in your life. As a Witch, you can use your knowledge of the power of words to craft magick and improve your world and the world around you. May you do so wisely and with great success.

Something to Try:

1) Create some Words of Power for one of your goals. Light a candle on your altar and say them every night for a month. Make note of any improvement in your situation.

2) On the left side of a sheet of paper, write down all the negative words you say about yourself. (If necessary, ask a friend to help you come up with the words you might not be aware of, or take a few days to listen which ones you use.) On the right side of the paper, write down positive replacements. Concentrate for a few minutes on your intention to let go of the negative and embrace the positive. Then tear the sheet of paper in half. Burn the list of negative words, bury them in the ground, or tear them up and flush them. Get rid of them in whatever way seems the most

powerful to you. Then put the list of positive words on your altar or somewhere else where you will see them often, and say them out loud every time you walk past them.

....

1   Fitch, *Magical Rites from the Crystal Well.*
2   Ibid., 52.
3   Weinstein, *Positive Magic.*
4   Ibid., 203.
5   Ibid., 214.

part two

the
inner
WITCH

Conscious Living

Integrating Your Spiritual Beliefs into Your Everyday Life

When I was younger, I used to daydream about being a White Witch. I pictured myself living in a quaint cottage in the middle of the woods. The beams of the kitchen would be hung with drying herbs, a healing potion would be boiling in a cauldron over the fire. Cats would be perched on the rocking chair in the corner and gaze out the window at the neatly laid-out gardens bursting with vegetables and magickal herbs. Solitary and serene, the only time this quiet existence would be broken was when someone would wander up the long path to my house seeking a healing salve, a spell, or a glimpse into the future. Ah, the perfect life of the ideal Witch.

Needless to say, the life I lead today doesn't bear much resemblance to this mystical, magickal ideal.

The gardens are there (although they're not all that neat), and the old farmhouse I live in might be considered quaint by some, even though it is missing the fireplace and the kitchen is usefully modern. And there are cats. Five of them, if you must know.

But solitary and serene it is not!

The women of my circle are in and out, both for formal celebrations of sabbats and esbats and just to connect over the course of our day-to-day lives. And while I do get calls for tarot readings, energy healings, and even the occasional spell, when the phone rings it's much more likely to be someone from work wanting me to fix a problem with the schedule, my editor needing to confer about a book I'm working on, or—Goddess forbid—a telemarketer.

My life is full of the mundane. Much of my time and energy goes to managing the minutiae of everyday survival: working, buying groceries, cleaning the house, working in the garden, and answering e-mails.

It is hardly the romantic life of the Witch that I imagined all those years ago. And yet, it is not so different from that vision as you might think.

You see, the ideal of that dream of a magickal life was to be a Witch all day, every day. And that is exactly what I am. I may not always wear the flowing dress and hooded cloak, but being a Witch has affected every aspect of my life, changing my thoughts, actions, and the attitude with which I approach all things, both magickal and mundane.

Like most modern Witches, I have chosen to live in the mundane world rather than to retreat from it into a fantasy existence based on a long-ago past. (As tempting as that can be some days.) But unlike the Pagans you may have met who only seem to remember that they are Witches on Beltane and Samhain, I try to bring my identity as a Witch to everything I do.

I believe that being a Witch is as much a way of life as it is a religion, and I strive to integrate the philosophy and values of Witchcraft into my ordinary life. In short, I am an Everyday Witch. And if you are reading this book, my guess is that you want to be one, too.

The chapters that follow are full of practical suggestions for ways that you can integrate your spiritual beliefs as a Witch into your everyday existence and hopefully create the kind of life that makes you glad to be a Witch—all day, every day.

Not all the issues will apply to everyone who reads the book, of course, and not all the advice, suggestions, or approaches will be right for you. Take what works for you, and ignore all the rest. I promise, you won't hurt my feelings.

The point is to make the most of all that being a Witch can bring to your life and to find new ways to "walk your talk" as a modern, magickal Everyday Witch.

Something to Think About:

Spend some time considering what aspects of your beliefs as a
Witch you wish to bring further into your mundane life and what
parts of your life most need a magickal boost. If you want, you can
write a list so that you have a clearer idea of what goals to focus on
as you read the rest of this book.

The Healthy Witch

Everybody wants to be healthy. We want to look good, feel good, and avoid illness—preferably without having to invest too much of our limited time and hard-won money in the process, or having to give up eating cookies and ice cream. This is true, at least in general, for everyone I know, no matter what his or her religion.

So what makes this different for someone who is a Witch? I think it comes down to three things: attitude, approach, and tools.

As Witches, we may look at the word "healthy" in a broader sense than most people, including mental and spiritual health as necessary components of what it means to be a healthy person. We are more likely to use nontraditional approaches, like herbs and energy work (such as Reiki and Therapeutic Touch), to treat physical problems or even to prevent them from happening in the first place. And, of course, we can use spells and rituals to deal with health issues, just as we use them for other goals, such as prosperity and love. This gives us "tools" to use in our pursuit of health that are not available to the rest of the population.

This chapter contains suggestions on how to use these three aspects of Witchcraft—attitude, approach, and tools—to aid your efforts to become a healthier Witch. For some people, this will primarily mean working on maintaining ongoing good health. For others, it will be the more challenging task of attempting to improve or put an end to already existing health problems.

In either case, remember that anything you find in this book is a general suggestion that may or may not be helpful in your particular situation and that not all things will work for all people. By all means, try the approach that feels right to you, but always use common sense and have reasonable expectations. That is to say, don't stop going to the doctor just because you've discovered a neat new herb, don't try lots of new things at once (which not only makes it impossible to tell which component is working but also increases the chances of having a bad reaction to something), and don't expect miraculous overnight results. While miracles certainly do happen (and I don't think you should rule out the possibility of one happening to you!), in reality the solutions to most health issues require time and persistence—and, just maybe, a little help from the gods.

Attitude

As with all other things Pagan, much of a Witch's attitude toward health stems from our basic spiritual beliefs. Take, for instance, the central core of Wicca, the Wiccan Rede. Eight simple words: *An' it harm none, do as ye will.*

As we have discussed elsewhere in this book, this phrase is not nearly as simple as it looks. When we say "harm none," that also includes ourselves. In theory, this means that no Witch should ever do anything that would cause him- or herself harm. That includes such unhealthy practices as smoking, drinking to excess, eating junk food, not getting enough sleep, spending all of our time on the couch instead of exercising, and even working at jobs that are stressful and soul-sapping.

In reality, of course, these things are not so easy to avoid. Old habits can be hard to let go of, even when we are aware of how bad for us they are. The unavoidable complications of everyday life and the realities of sharing your space with significant others, kids, roommates, and pets can throw obstacles into the path of the best-intentioned plans. And most of us have to work for a living, whether we like it or not.

Does this mean that there is no point in trying to be healthy? Of course not. For one thing, without our health, it becomes increasingly difficult—if not downright impossible—to manage all of those everyday complications. So we owe it to ourselves and to those with whom we share our lives to be as healthy as we possibly can be. But more than this, I believe that as Witches we have an obligation to strive always to be the best that we can be and to truly follow the intent of "harm none." We may sometimes fall short of our goal, but the genuine intention and attempt to be the best human beings that we can be is central to being a Witch.

So give it your best shot. And even if you sometimes fail, keep trying. Allow yourself to be human and (just occasionally) imperfect, but also believe that you are capable of achieving anything you truly desire, including living a healthy and balanced life.

Remember that in Witchcraft *intent* is crucial. If you really decide to be a healthier, happier person, you can be. The gods believe in you. I believe in you. You just have to believe in yourself.

What are some of the other attitudes and beliefs that most Witches share that have an effect on health and healing? Of course, the fact that Wicca is a nature-based religion is a central factor in the way many Pagans look at illness. Rather than seeing sickness as an isolated problem, we are aware that it is usually a symptom of a lack of balance somewhere in our bodies or in our lives. Dis-ease, meaning a lack of ease somewhere, is often the cause of what modern medicine might view as a purely physical problem.

Just as a plant in a garden will demonstrate its lack of a crucial nutrient by drooping, so too will our bodies show signs of a lack of something we need—or too much of something we don't need—by manifesting symptoms. It's telling us there is a problem. It's our job to stay alert for these signs (not always an easy task when life is rushed and overflowing) and to try and find a way to return our bodies to balance.

Witches are also more likely to place importance on the mind-body connection. Since the beginning of time, Pagans have known about the influence the mind has on the body, and vice versa, although the modern medical community is only starting to take this into consideration.

Most Pagan cultures had someone in the community in the position of shaman or witch doctor. These folks not only cared for their patients' physical needs but for their spiritual ones as well, often treating obvious physical symptoms by addressing the spiritual issues they believed were at the root of the problem. In Native American society, the shaman was said to walk "the healing way," and modern-day Pagans often look to the Pagan cultures that preceded us for ideas to help us on our own healing paths.

This can mean going to counseling or seeking advice from a high priest, high priestess, or a respected elder. It may also mean listening to your guides, whether that is a guardian spirit or that little voice in the back of your head.

Another key tenet in Wiccan beliefs is that of personal responsibility. Just as no one else can be responsible for our success or failure in other aspects of our lives, likewise no one else can be responsible for our health. For example, while it is easy to blame stress on a job or a loved one, it is important to remember that only you can choose how you deal with that stress or whether any particular situation is worth the stress it causes you.

By taking on the responsibility for our own lives, we also reclaim our own power to bring about change. If others cause the problems, there may be nothing we can do to fix those problems. But if we are ultimately responsible for our own lives, then we have the ability to change those aspects of our lives that cause us harm.

Does this mean that if you are sick it is your own fault? Not necessarily. In fact, we are often given illnesses that make no sense to us and that are not caused in any obvious way by our lifestyles or choices. A bad diet or lack of exercise certainly doesn't cause multiple sclerosis, for instance. And even the people who lead the healthiest lives can end up with cancer or heart problems.

Some people believe that all illness has at its root some imbalance in the body, heart, or soul, maybe something that goes back even as far as a previous life. Personally, I'm not sure it is always possible to tell where some illnesses begin; sometimes the best you can do is deal with whatever it is that is facing you, no matter where it came from.

Whatever problems you are confronting—whether it is a serious illness or ongoing everyday challenges, from weight gain to hot flashes—remember that the manner with which you approach these difficulties is of enormous importance.

A positive attitude is often the difference between success and failure, and believing that a problem can be solved can be the first step to solving it. So no matter what health issues you face, it is important to focus on being as positive as possible. Have the intent to heal yourself (both by what you do and by seeking out those who can best help you), and know in your heart that there are forces in the universe that are willing to aid you in becoming a healthier, stronger Witch. In the end, "to will, to know, and to do" are as much core ideas in dealing with your health as they are when practicing magick.

Approach

How you deal with the common cold can be a pretty good indication of how you might deal with a more serious illness. So here is a short quiz to give you an idea of what your approach might be:

1. Ignore it—eventually it will go away.

2. Go to the doctor and insist he give you an antibiotic.

3. Take every over-the-counter cold medicine there is and go to bed for a week.

4. Eat an orange, take some echinacea, suck on zinc lozenges, eat a lot of garlic, drink lots of hot peppermint or ginger tea, and rest as much as you can, given your hectic schedule. Take cold medicine if you have to, in moderation. And maybe a little chicken soup.

Mind you, none of these are wrong, necessarily (well, okay, except for the second one—antibiotics have no effect on colds), but they do all demonstrate different approaches to illness.

The first approach (the "tough it out" method) may work some of the time. But ignoring small problems with your body often leads to bigger ones. You might be able to tough out a cold by simply going on the way you normally do, but sometimes that leads to complications like pneumonia or bronchitis. At the very least, it will probably mean that the cold will hang on longer than it would have if you had let your body have the rest and support it needed.

The second approach (the "magick bullet" method) is handing your illness over to some doctor and expecting him or her to fix it with no active participation on your part. Not only are you likely to end up taking a lot of expensive medicines that you don't need, but most of the time this method simply doesn't work. In fact, you can often end up with bigger problems than the ones you started out with in the first place.

Don't get me wrong—I have nothing against doctors or modern medicine. (Well, hardly anything, anyway.) In many circumstances, going to a doctor is the right answer. If you break your leg, for instance, I would certainly head there first. What you do after the doctor puts on a cast…well, now, that can make all the difference. But we'll get to that in a minute.

The third approach (the "Band-Aid" method) might work. And depending on the cold, it isn't necessarily a bad option. On the other hand, most of us can't afford to stay in bed for a week, and many over-the-counter medicines have side effects you don't want. More than that, though, they don't do anything to solve the problem; all they do is cover up the symptoms. And while sometimes that is all you want in the short term, in the long term, that probably isn't the best solution.

Approach number four, on the other hand, does something that the other three don't: it actually gives your body the ammunition it needs to fight off the cold faster and with less unpleasant fall-out. You might use a few modern inventions or even a recipe handed down by your mom, but you will also rely on proven alternative remedies, folk medicine, and good old common sense.

We'll call this the "healthy Witch" approach. The healthy Witch is in charge of her (or his) own health. She pays attention when her body sends signals that indicate some sort of malfunction. She uses all the tools at her disposal—including modern medicine but also exploring the options of more nontraditional approaches, like herbal medicine, acupuncture, hypnotherapy, energy healing, aromatherapy, and the like. She never forgets the importance of basics like diet and exercise and is willing to put in the time and effort it takes to maintain a healthy lifestyle—even if some days, that just means going to bed with a cup of tea and a box of tissues.

What does this signify for a health problem more serious than the common cold? I'll give you an example out of my own life. I have something called fibromyalgia. It's a pain in the butt...and everywhere else. Essentially, it is a condition that causes a great deal of muscle and joint pain. Modern science has a few theories, but the truth is that they don't know what causes it or how to treat it. All they can do is give a patient pain medicine and sometimes antidepressants. There is no cure, and once you've got it, you probably have it for life.

When I was originally diagnosed many years ago, I tried a few of the possible medical treatments, none of which helped, and I took *a lot* of painkillers. Eventually I got tired of being told that there was nothing I could do, and I did some things.

I increased my exercise and improved my diet. I tried massage and acupuncture and Reiki and hypnotherapy, along with various natural supplements. None of those things turned out to be a miracle cure, but they all helped. Do I still have fibromyalgia? Yes, I do. Do I still take pain medicine? Occasionally, on a really bad day.

The difference is that while this condition still has an effect on my life, it no longer rules me. I know I'm doing everything I can to find a solution, and that I'm doing my best to be in charge of my own physical well-being. I fully intend to keep looking for ways to improve my health.

This is what it means to follow the "healthy Witch" approach. You use all the tools available to you, take responsibility for your own body, and do the best you can.

Tools

Once you get past the basics of modern medicine, you will discover that there are any number of options for alternative healing techniques, ranging from the ancient (acupuncture) to the New Age (high colonics). Some are more appealing than others, needless to say, and not all of them are suitable for every condition.

But among all of these alternatives, there are four in particular that are of special interest and relevance to Witches: herbs, energy healing, the mind-body connection, and magick.

Herbs

Pagans have been using herbs, in all their varied forms, since before the beginning of recorded time. Egyptian pharaohs were buried with them, Druids used them in their religious practices, and healers throughout the centuries have utilized herbs to treat everything from headaches to the pangs of childbirth.

Many of today's modern medicines were originally derived from herbs; aspirin comes from white willow tree bark, for instance, and digitalis (a heart medicine) from the foxglove plant. And although the modern versions of some ancient remedies might come in more convenient packages, that doesn't mean that herbal remedies have no place in the medicine chest of the Everyday Witch.

Take our example of the common cold. (No, seriously—*you* take it, I don't want it!) Caused by a virus, the symptoms often include a stuffed or runny nose, sore throat, achy body, and a feeling of exhaustion. The modern medical approach is to treat the symptoms with decongestants (which clear your head but can leave you jumpy), antihistamines (which can make you sleepy), and painkillers like aspirin or ibuprofen (which can bother your stomach).

Now don't get me wrong—I'm not telling you *not* to use these things; if they work for you, by all means go ahead. But you may want to add some remedies from your herbal toolbox as well.

For instance, ginger is a natural anti-inflammatory, as well as being a "heating" herb. So drinking ginger tea may ease your aches and open up your sinuses while giving you the added benefit of increasing your fluid intake. (Don't forget what your mother said about drinking lots of hot liquids when you are sick.)

Eucalyptus is another herb that is great for clearing away congestion. Try taking a hot bath with a few drops of eucalyptus essential oil or inhaling the steam from a bowl of hot water with the oil added to it. Did your mother slather your chest with Vicks vapor rub when you were a child? One of the active ingredients in this useful classic is menthol, which is derived from peppermint.

Herbal remedies come in a variety of different forms, including essential oils, tinctures, teas, pills, and the fresh or dried herbs themselves. They can also be used as homeopathics or flower essences, where the essence of the plant is distilled down into a tiny but potent amount.

There are many fabulous books on the medicinal uses of herbs, so I am not going to spend a lot of time here going into the details of every herbal medicine available. Suffice it to say that, like the Witch of days gone by, the modern Witch can also be well served by using herbs as a healing tool.

Just remember to do your research well, avoid any dangerous herbs (such as foxglove), and experiment cautiously. Like the other tools we use, herbs can be quite powerful and must be handled with care.

On the positive side, they are often readily available (you can even grow your own), are less expensive than prescription medicines, and are a potent ally in your efforts to be a healthy Witch. What's more, they can be used in combination with magick and spellcraft, and nobody ever said that about an aspirin, as far as I know!

Energy Healing

Energy healing is a broad term that covers modalities from acupuncture (where needles are placed at specific points on the body in order to move or balance the *chi*, or energy) to Therapeutic Touch (an ironic name, since the practitioner moves the body's energy by adjusting the energy fields that lie about an inch above the skin without actually touching the patient).

Over time, Pagan healers, shamans, and medicine people have historically used a variety of techniques to adjust their patient's energy or to draw on the universal energy around them, or both. Depending on the culture, this energy may be seen as coming from the healer herself, from the surrounding universe, or directly from a god or goddess.

Christians sometimes referred to this as the laying-on of hands, and others might call it psychic healing. No matter what it is labeled, energy healing can be a powerful tool, especially in addressing physical issues for which modern medicine has no solutions.

Reiki is perhaps the best known of the popular types of energy healing. The word translates to "universal life force" and is a form of energy healing that originated in Japan. Reiki is passed down through classes and attunements given by those who have reached the highest level of training, known as Reiki Masters.

Therapeutic Touch, a type of energy healing that began in the nursing community, is another technique used to manipulate the energy fields of the body. Also taught in classes, Therapeutic Touch greatly resembles Reiki except that, in general, its practitioners work with their hands a few inches away from the body instead of putting their hands directly on the patient.

In essence, both these methods channel energy from the universe through the practitioner and into the client. Although the energy worker acts as a skilled conduit, he or she is only facilitating; the patient's body is actually healing itself. The most powerful healers are masters at channeling this energy.

I do a type of healing that I refer to as Intuitive Energy Healing. The only real difference between what I do and Reiki or Therapeutic Touch is that my abilities came to me as a gift, as opposed to being taught to me by someone else. In fact, I have studied both of these modalities, mostly because I was curious to see if there was any real difference between the kind of energy that I manipulate and that used in the other forms.

As far as I can tell, all three kinds of healing are essentially the same—the energy used by the practitioner is identical, only the techniques are different. Over the course of time, I have adopted bits and pieces of Reiki, Therapeutic Touch, and various other systems of healing. In short, I use anything that works to help my clients.

Here's another example from my own life. One of my sisters has had persistent problems with her eyes, and a couple of years ago she was told that she had a hole in the back of her retina, and that if the hole got any larger, she would have to have surgery. She was also told that it was most likely that the hole would, in fact, get larger. She made an appointment for a date a couple of months later to recheck the eye and arrange for the surgery.

About a week before her appointment, I happened to be visiting. When she told me about the problem, I did energy work on the eye for about an hour. It was one of those rare sessions during which I could really feel the *oomph* that comes when the energy is flowing unusually well. In the week following our session, she called to tell me that her vision seemed somewhat better—definitely a good sign.

When she went to her appointment, a technician placed her at a machine that would help them view the inside of the eye. My sister told me afterward that he looked twice, checked her file, looked again, and then went to fetch the doctor, saying that he thought perhaps they had the wrong records. The doctor came in, looked at her eye, rechecked her file, and shook his head in amazement.

He had no explanation, he told her, but the hole was much smaller. Surgery was postponed indefinitely. Needless to say, my sister was pretty happy, and so was I.

Now mind you, this is a pretty dramatic example. (Well, heck, that's why I'm using it, after all.) It is unusual to have this radical an improvement after only one session, no matter how powerful the healer might be. I have no way of knowing how much this outcome was affected by my close personal connection to the patient, her faith in me, or the fervent prayers I sent out to the gods while I worked on her.

The point is, it worked.

What does this mean to you, the Witch in search of healing?

Actually, it means two things: one, that any true energy healer can probably help you feel better, and two, that you can probably learn some form of energy healing that you can use either on yourself or others.

We all have the ability to manipulate our own energy to one degree or another. If you want to see what I mean, try the following simple experiment: hold your hands out comfortably in front of you, palms facing each other, about eight inches apart. Visualize a ball of energy floating between your two hands. Move your hands slowly toward each other. As they get closer, you will feel a slight resistance. What you're feeling is energy.

Once you've done this a few times and can really feel that ball of energy between your hands, you can go to the next step. Take that energy and visualize holding it in the palm of one hand. Now hold that hand a couple of inches away from the opposite shoulder and run it slowly down the length of your arm. If you are concentrating, you can probably feel the energy moving as your hand moves.

Don't worry if you don't succeed at this right away; not everyone has the same degree of natural ability in this area. Just keep practicing; it will eventually come to you.

Once you learn to manipulate this energy, you can use it to help heal some of life's little aches and pains. Try it the next time you bump your knee or have an upset stomach, and see if gathering up that ball of energy and holding it on the spot that's bothering you makes you feel better. Then try it on someone you love.

There are a couple of aspects of energy healing that you need to keep in mind. First, like any other type of healing (including modern medicine), some people are better at it than others. And there are always those who will say that they are gifted when they are not. Try to get recommendations from others when choosing an energy healer, and always pay attention to your own intuition. Beware of those charging absurd amounts of money or claiming to work miracles.

Second, if and when you learn to do energy healing yourself, be aware that not everyone is open to this type of healing—or, in fact, to being healed at all. You can offer, but be prepared to be gracious if people say no, thank you. Many Pagans use their energy healing abilities only on themselves, and that's just fine.

The Mind-Body Connection

Energy healing is often used in conjunction with what is known as the mind-body connection. At its simplest, this means that the mind and the body are tied inseparably together, and that one affects the other in ways that we are only beginning to understand.

Witches use a variety of mind-body systems, including hypnotherapy (which may entail self-hypnosis or even past-life regression), shamanic journeying, visualization, and meditation. The positive affirmations we talked about earlier would also fall into this category.

Shamans and other Pagan healers have traditionally used the relationship between mind and body to aid in healing. Much of the ritual associated with witch doctors, shamans, and the like was intended in part to convince the patient that the medicine was working, and it was as vital an ingredient as any herb. Our own magickal rituals can also be used as an aid in healing, especially when they are used in conjunction with other therapeutic tools.

In and of itself, belief is possibly the most powerful healing tool of them all. You may have heard of what modern medicine calls the placebo effect. This happens when the placebo (usually a sugar pill with no active ingredients) has the same effect as an actual medicine.

For instance, if twenty patients in a study testing a new painkiller are given a sugar pill and told that it is a powerful new medicine, four or five of them may report that their pain was significantly lessened (regardless of the fact that the pill they were given had no medicinal properties at all).

So why did the sugar pill work as if it were real medication? Because they believed it would. A person in authority (a doctor or scientist) told them this "medicine" would cure their pain, and because the patients believed in the doctor, they also believed in the medicine. Their belief was so strong, it caused the pill to work as if it were a genuine cure.

Of course, the downside of belief is that if people are told that they will not get well (and they have faith in the authority figure who tells them so), that belief will also affect the outcome of their illness. This is where the power of "cursing" comes from; it is as much a matter of the person believing the curse will work as it is the ability of the person who cast it.

Dr. Andrew Weil, a popular author and physician who argues for the inclusion of herbs and a focus on the mind-body connection in the practice of modern medicine, invented a term that he calls "medical hexing." (And just a note: he is a good person to read if you are looking for a way to integrate the old and new forms of healing.)

"Medical hexing" occurs when a doctor gives a patient a negative diagnosis, such as "you'll be dead in a year" or "there is no cure, you will have this condition forever," and the patient believes it to the extent that it becomes true. Essentially, the modern doctor has "cursed" the patient, just as a witch doctor might have done in days gone by. (1)

This is not to say that doctors aren't often correct when they give a patient bad news or that the patient isn't entitled to the doctor's opinion. But if you are given such a diagnosis, keep in mind that it is just that: an opinion, an educated guess based on statistics and the doctor's training and experience, which hopefully are vast but which may not take into consideration all the factors, including that of the patient's will to get better.

Again, I'm not suggesting that you ignore a doctor's advice. But don't necessarily just accept bad news and give up, either. Remember that the power of your own belief and the additional tools that Witches have to draw on in times of difficulty can make a remarkable amount of difference.

Various studies have shown the importance of the mind-body connection in both maintaining wellness and resolving illness. Reports have demonstrated the benefits of everything from using laughter as a part of therapy to the power of positive thought. They are solid support for the "healthy Witch" approach to health.

Our belief in the unseen world around us often leads us to use tools such as shamanic journeying, soul retrieval, or past-life regression in order to explore the possible roots of a physical or emotional problem that may not be obvious on the surface.

Certainly, I can tell you that when I went to a hypnotherapist for help with my own physical issues, intending to try to steer my body away from pain on a subconscious level, I got way more than I'd been looking for. As it happened, I was lucky enough to be guided to one of the most powerful healers I have ever met, who in addition to being a hypnotherapist was also a Pagan trained in shamanic practices (as well as being a PhD).

Together, we took many remarkable journeys into the hidden pathways of my mind and spirit, and much of this deep interior work revealed answers to the whys and wherefores of my exterior physical problems. It was an amazing and often soul-shaking experience, and one that forever changed who I am and what I believe. It also had the unexpected benefit of reinforcing my growing Pagan beliefs.

While it is helpful to have a guide such as a hypnotherapist or a shaman, many Pagans undertake this type of journeying on their own. There is no reason why you cannot do the same if you are not fortunate enough to have an expert at hand. And even if you are not battling an illness, any path that leads to further enlightenment is one worth following, as long as it is done with care.

Most Pagans believe in reincarnation—that we all live many lives in the course of our time here on Mother Earth. The purpose of these multiple existences is to give us repeated opportunities to learn and grow and to become the best, highest selves we can be. Exploring the mind-body connection can be yet another step toward self-knowledge and self-improvement.

Of course, there are also less-complicated methods of using the mind-body connection to heal ourselves. One way of integrating the mind with the power of another tool—energy healing—is by using visualization.

Visualization is a simple process that uses the power of the mind to influence the body. (It can also be used in conjunction with magick, and often is. As Witches, the tools that we use for the physical and for the metaphysical are often the same.) When coupled with energy healing, visualization can become an even more potent tool in our nontraditional medicine kit.

You will find a simple visualization exercise at the end of the chapter, if you want to see what I mean. There are also many good books available that explore the area of mind-body connection, as well as a large variety of guided meditation tapes, some of which are aimed at specific medical problems.

As Pagans, in addition to having these valuable tools at our disposal, it is possible for us to give the negative aspects of illness something of a positive spin. I know, you're saying to yourself, "What the heck is she talking about…is she nuts?" How can being sick be a good thing?

Well, obviously, in many cases it isn't. But illness can also be a journey to knowledge, self-improvement, and positive change.

Sometimes we get sick because we have unhealthy habits, and—usually by giving us a swift kick in the butt—the illness helps us change to habits that are more beneficial. If we need an all-encompassing change to get out of a bad relationship, to switch jobs or careers, or to alter the way in which we view the world, illness can help us achieve that, too. But we must pay attention to the messages our bodies are sending us.

Sickness of the body is not fun, but it can often be a signpost that can point us to an underlying illness of the mind or spirit that we can address through the power of the mind-body connection. And as Witches, we know that our minds are the most powerful tools of all.

Magick

We use magick to improve our lives in many ways. There are entire books, for instance, that focus on spells for love or prosperity; you may even own a few. But when we are dealing with issues involving our health, we often forget to use this powerful tool.

Perhaps that's because, at least in part, there may be many more obvious solutions that work as well or better; you wouldn't do magick to get rid of a cold, after all. And additionally, it can be hard to gather the focus you need to work magick when you are not feeling your best.

Certainly, magick isn't always the best way to go. But what if you are dealing with chronic issues, such as a long-term illness or stubborn bad habits you just can't seem to let go of, even though you know they are having a negative affect on your health?

When dealing with issues such as these, you have the opportunity to act as your own personal "witch doctor," if you'll excuse the term. Magick can be a potent asset in your quest for healing, especially if you combine it with other tools like herbs or visualization.

Our belief in the power of words is a major component of magick, and we use that power when we work spells for healing or anything else. But spells are not the only option to consider when using words for healing purposes.

For instance, I sometimes take pain medications, which can be hard on both the stomach and the liver. On the mundane level, I take practical measures to avoid these side effects; I make sure I have food in my stomach when I take the medications, and I don't combine them with alcohol, which can worsen both symptoms. But on the magickal level, I take one more step to protect myself—I say a blessing over the pills before I swallow them.

This may seem peculiar, but think about the power of words, and then look at what this particular blessing says:

> *Help this medicine with its task*
> *To do its work as I doth ask*
> *Remove the pain both weak and strong*
> *Working swift and lasting long*
> *Cause no harm or ill effect*
> *While my health it does protect*

If you think back to our discussion in chapter three about the ability of words to change the molecular structure of an object, then you can see that it might be possible to negate or at least lessen some of the more destructive properties associated with this medicine by saying such a blessing.

While I still want to take as few pills as possible, using the power of words may help to protect me from harm when I do take them. You can see that I am clearly spelling out what I want the magick to do: help the medicine work to the best of its ability while also curtailing any damage it might otherwise cause.

This sort of blessing can be adapted for use with any number of different medications or treatments. It uses magickal tools as an adjunct to modern medicine.

You can also use Marion Weinstein's Words of Power format (also in chapter three) when dealing with health issues. For instance, you could say:

> *There is One Power*
> *And this Power is perfect health.*
> *And I, _____, am a perfect manifestation of this Power.*
> *Therefore, perfect health is mine, here and now.*
> *For the good of all, and according to free will,*
> *And so it must be.*

Last but not least, you could use a spell to help you achieve the goal of improving your health or reducing bad habits.

For instance, there are many herbs that are used both medicinally and magickally, so you could write a spell that utilizes peppermint and then drink the magickally charged herb as a tea. In this way, you get the healthful qualities of the peppermint along with an added boost from the spell. (Remember: never take an herb internally without checking from a reputable source first to be sure it is safe.)

You could also write a spell to address your particular health problem, or use a general healing spell like the one I've included here. For healing spells, you probably want to put on some soothing background music (maybe even a special "Reiki music" or "healing music" CD). Cast your circle to create sacred space, and call upon the deities of your choice. Good god/desses to ask for help with healing include Artemis, Athena, Brigid, Hygeia, Inanna, Isis, Sekmet, Minerva, Asclepius, Apollo, Paeon, Thoth, and Vishnu, among others. Dab a blue candle with any healing magickal oil, and light it while sending out this spell:

> *I call upon the gods above*
> *In perfect trust, in perfect love*
> *I ask for health and energy*
> *Balanced and in synergy*
> *Healthy body, mind, and soul*
> *A perfect balanced, healthy whole*
> *I pledge that I will do my part*
> *For healthy body, healthy heart*
> *Every day let health increase*
> *Until all signs of illness cease*

Then spend some time visualizing yourself as healthy and whole. You may want to send a golden healing light to surround the problem area while you are at it.

This type of spell would probably be done during the full moon or during the time of the waxing moon, since you are trying to bring in health. Another approach, more likely done during the new moon or the time of the waning moon, would be to do a spell to banish illness. Feel free to use this one if you like it. The instructions are essentially the same as for the first healing spell, although since you are doing banishing magick, you can substitute a black or dark blue candle if you wish.

> I *call upon the powers given*
> By *the new moon, dark and strong*
> I *banish, strip, and wash away*
> All *those things that don't belong*
> I *banish illness, pain, and weakness*
> I *banish struggle without gain*
> I *banish all those not of lightness*
> And *forbid them come again*
> I *bind and banish three times three*
> And *as I will, so mote it be*

When you are finished saying the spell, spend some time with a visualization to remove the health problem. One good technique is to see a golden net of light passing down through your body, starting at the top of your head and moving down, scooping up all negativity and dis-ease as it goes. You may need to spend more time on the problem areas. Be sure to send all that nasty stuff harmlessly out into the universe when you're done.

The important point here is to use every tool you have at your disposal when dealing with issues of health, including all those that can be found in the Everyday Witch's magickal medicine chest.

Something to Think About:

1) Which of these four approaches discussed in this chapter most closely represents the way you deal with illness? Is it working for you? If not, what can you do to change it?

2) If you are having problems with your health, consider what your illness might be trying to teach you. Is your body asking you to change your habits or lifestyle? If so, are you listening to it or ignoring it?

Something to Try:

Write out some Words of Power or a spell for healing. Whichever you choose, recite it every day for two weeks, and see what happens.

....
1 Weil, *Spontaneous Healing*, 61.

Mindful Eating

Witches love good food. It is a way to show appreciation for the bounty of the earth and to celebrate the blessings in our lives. And no feast would be complete without some self-indulgent comfort food and sweet desserts.

So how do we draw the line between what feeds the soul and what feeds the body—and do we even have to? We all want to eat well. But what does that mean, exactly? If you are a Pagan, there is more to the concept of eating well than just eating a healthy, well-balanced diet, although that's important, too. (And no, fries in one hand and a brownie in the other is not the kind of balance I am talking about here.)

For Witches, with our strong connection to nature, it is as important to eat mindfully as it is to eat healthily. Mindful eating means not only taking care to eat foods that are good for you but also paying attention to how you eat them and where they come from.

Awareness and Appreciation

For our ancestors who lived on the land, it was easy to remain conscious of the day-to-day origins of the food they ate; after all, they were the ones doing the hunting, gathering, planting, and harvesting.

But for those of us who get our food primarily in sterile packages from large grocery stores, it can be very difficult to make the connection between the food on our plates and the fields, streams, or animals from which it came.

To me, mindful eating includes being aware of what went into getting what I eat from its place of origin to my dining-room table. Once you start paying attention to where your food comes from, you may want to change the way you eat.

For instance, how far does your food travel to reach you? Much of what we eat today is not grown anywhere near us. Fruits and vegetables that come from out of the country or across many states are often raised specifically to hold up to the strains of long-distance travel. What appears to be fresh when you see it in the store is often, in fact, many weeks old. Furthermore, food that is transported hundreds or thousands of miles can be tough on the environment in terms of the amount of fuel it takes to ship it, and it may require more pesticides and preservatives.

Many Pagans are trying to be more conscious of where their food comes from, buying locally raised produce and meat when they can, and eating the foods naturally in season locally during any particular time of the year. This has the added benefit of supporting local farmers and putting fresher, more nutritious food on your table.

Of course, the best way to make a connection with the food you eat is to grow some of it yourself. If nothing else, having a garden and raising your own vegetables helps you tune in to the seasonal changes and gives you an appreciation for how much work it takes to produce a single tomato. In addition, when you grow your own food, you can control what goes into your soil or onto the plants. Most, although not all, Witches try to keep their gardens as close to organic as they can.

Even if you can't have a garden of your own, you can try to be more aware of where your food comes from and maintain an attitude of conscious appreciation and gratitude for the work and sacrifices that go into feeding you.

Some Pagans say a blessing over their food before they eat in an effort to remind themselves to be grateful and as a way of expressing that gratitude to Mother Earth. You can try saying something like the following:

I give thanks for the food before me, gifts of the earth, and I eat it with appreciation and gratitude for all that it took to provide it for me. May it help me to be healthy and strong. So mote it be.

There are Witches who feel that it is better not to eat meat because of the strong connection between us and the animals who share the earth with us. Others feel that consuming meat is a part of the never-ending cycle of life and death. There is no right or wrong answer here; each of us has to make that decision for ourselves.

What I do believe, however, is that those of us who choose to eat meat need to do so with appreciation for the sacrifice that has been made. I was a vegetarian for about eight years. These days I eat some meat, although it is not a major part of my diet. On those occasions when I do eat it, I always try to take a moment to say thank you to the animal that died so that I might continue to live.

Part of my attitude is colored by an experience I had when I first went back to eating meat after many years of being a vegetarian. This was only a few years into my Pagan practice, and I was still feeling my way in many areas, including this one. I ran into an interesting question of ethics in the process. It turns out that my power animal is a flock of sheep. (Seriously. Yes, I was hoping for something powerful and dignified like a hawk or a wolf. I got a flock of sheep. Please stop laughing now.)

So here was the question: Is it really bad karma to eat your power animal? One of my favorite kinds of meat was lamb. But was it against some kind of rule to still eat it? To be honest, I thought it probably was. But to find out for sure, I asked my power animals directly the next time I was in a trance state. The answer I got surprised me.

I was told, "We would be honored to help support your body." (One of the ways you can tell if the answer to a question comes from outside as opposed to inside is that the answer is completely different from the one you were expecting.) And so I do occasionally eat lamb, but always with gratitude and respect.

None of us can eat the perfect diet all the time. It is often a matter of compromising between eating healthy and the very real limits on the amount of time and money we have to put toward our food. As Pagans, however, we need to try to add our connection to nature into the equation as often as we can.

Food as Celebration

One of the great things about celebrating the sabbats with other Witches, at least for me, is the feast that usually follows the ritual. For one thing, our love of food (and of feeding each other) often results in a truly spectacular array of edibles. But more than that, and the main reason for the feast, is that Pagans have traditionally celebrated the turning of the Wheel of the Year with foods that reflect both the holiday and our appreciation of the earth's bounty.

The Pagans of days gone by followed the cycles of the year in everything they did; these cycles were as much a part of their lives as the rising and setting of the sun. Their close ties to, and dependence on, the land made them constantly aware of the seasonal changes and all that came with them. To these folks, a good harvest meant the difference between survival and starvation, and the first signs of spring signaled the beginning of the end of the lean times of winter. They celebrated with feasts to express their joy and to give thanks to the gods.

Few of today's Witches are at the mercy of the changing seasons in the ways that our ancestors were. But we still observe the eight holidays of the Wheel with feasts for the same reasons they did and additionally to strengthen our connection with the land and those who came before us.

Even if you are a Solitary Witch, you can make a special meal featuring the foods that are celebrated at that particular sabbat—for instance, bread at Lammas or milk at Imbolc. And if you are gathering with a group of fellow Witches, there is nothing better than a feast shared with those who share your joy and gratitude. And as everyone knows, there are no calories in the food we eat at feasts with other Pagans!

. . . .

Balance

The goal of eating mindfully is not so much a matter of trying to follow an impossible set of rules or never allowing ourselves food or drink we know is bad for us. After all, eating is not just a matter of taking in sustenance but also a joyful celebration of living our lives to the fullest.

Instead, eating mindfully is all about balance, as is much of everything else that we do in our lives as Everyday Witches. We try to balance the need for a healthy body with the limits placed on us by our often-hectic lives. We do our best to eat in a fashion that is good for both us and the earth, and we remember to be grateful.

After all, our bodies are a living manifestation of God and Goddess, and they deserve to be nurtured like the little piece of the divine that they are.

Something to Think About:

What is your favorite food? Do you know why it is your favorite? Does it most feed body or soul? Does it remind you of your childhood or some special occasion? Is it a healthy food?

Something to Try:

At the next sabbat, research the origins of the holiday and the types of foods that were traditionally served. Try to create a feast that features these foods in as healthy a way as possible.

Dealing with Crisis

How Does Being a Witch Help When Things Go Wrong?

One of my coven members recently asked me how she could best use her spiritual beliefs as a Witch to help her during a crisis. It was a question that really made me stop and think. After all, I knew that I was already doing this. But I'd actually never examined how I did it.

I have used Witchcraft and my beliefs as a Witch to cope with life's trials and tribulations, both large and small. But what was it about being a Witch that made me stronger and more capable of dealing with whatever the universe was throwing at me this week? It was a darned good question, and after I'd pondered it a while, this was what I came up with:

Faith

First and foremost, for me at least, being a Witch is about faith. Not just faith in the gods, although that is a biggie, but faith in myself as well. Since becoming a Pagan, I have developed a faith in my own abilities that I didn't have in earlier years.

Each of us struggles with our view of self during some point in our lives, some of us more than others. But if you are still alive and kicking, you can't be doing all that badly. And no matter how rough life's challenges might get, if you have faith in your own ability to triumph over adversity, you'll come through it all in the end.

But what if you're not all that sure of your own strength? That's where the other side of faith comes in.

I believe that the gods never send us more than we can truly bear. They may (and often do) send us more than we *think* we can bear, but whatever crisis has landed in our laps, it wouldn't be there if we couldn't deal with it. And when we feel as if we have reached the limit of our ability to cope, we can always ask the gods for help. Part of being a Witch is having faith that there is a powerful source for strength that we can draw upon during the most difficult times of our lives, whether it comes from the inside or the outside.

Learning and Growth

As Witches, most of us put a lot of emphasis on learning and growth. Our belief in personal responsibility means, among other things, that we are in charge of our own destiny in many ways, and so we strive to improve ourselves, both as Witches and as human beings. But there is no growth without change, and change is often brought about through coping with adversity.

I suspect that most of what we call "crisis" is sent to us as a learning experience and as an opportunity to learn and grow. This concept doesn't make the difficult times any more fun or easier to get through, but it does make me look at crisis in a different way—as a challenge instead of a curse. It is tempting to ask, "Why me?" when things get rough. Instead, try asking, "What am I supposed to be learning?" You might be surprised at how much difference this change in perspective can make.

Perspective

Being a Witch means that you often look at the world in different ways than the non-Pagan folks do. The Pagan perspective on life can often make a great difference when you are dealing with upheaval. If you take the above example, for instance, and you look upon a problem as an opportunity for learning rather than, say, a punishment for sin, you are more likely to try to create something productive out of the situation.

It is always a good idea to ask yourself this question: "How bad is this, really?" Many of us can get pretty bent out of shape by the everyday crap that life throws at us (and who can blame us, really…much of it is crap!). But if you step back for a moment and try to look at the problem with a bit of perspective, maybe you will discover that it isn't as bad as you think. My circle-sister Chris says, "It's not really a crisis unless someone is horribly hurt or dead." (She's a nurse, so you can see where her perspective on this comes from.)

And if someone dies, the belief that many Witches share in reincarnation can be a consolation as well. While the grief still runs deep, the knowledge that we will meet up with our loved ones again in another life can make our loss seem not quite so bad. As Pagans, we view life as an ever-turning circle, where nothing is ever truly lost. Death is only another turn of the Wheel and a part of the natural cycle of birth, growth, death, and rebirth.

Support

So, what if your crisis really is a crisis? Then, if you are a Pagan, you look for support in a few places that non-Pagans might not.

If you belong to a group, be it circle, coven, or grove, you can depend on your circle-mates to be there for you, come what may. (And if you can't, maybe you're in the wrong group.) My group has gotten together to support each other in times of crisis a number of times, sometimes at a moment's notice. Like family, that's what you're there for.

As a high priestess, I am often a source of support for members of my coven when they are struggling with a difficult situation. Even if you don't belong to a group, you may be able to find a local high priest or high priestess who would be willing to help out. I know that I would never turn away any fellow Pagan who came to me for comfort or advice, whether or not they happened to be a member of my group.

If you don't happen to know any other Pagans well enough to ask them for help, it is possible to find wisdom and support in books as well. Reading some of the deeper Pagan works, like Marion Weinstein's *Positive Magic*, can inspire and encourage a troubled Witch. There are also books that, while not Pagan per se, are close enough to our belief system that you might find them helpful. For instance, there is a wonderful Buddhist book called *When Things Fall Apart: Heart Advice for Difficult Times* by Pema Chodron (Shambhala Publishing, 1997), which is worth adding to any collection.

And of course you can turn to the gods for support, too. You can send up a prayer or simply talk out loud, and know that you are heard. They may not answer your prayer in the way you want, but if you open yourself to it, their love is always there to wrap around yourself like a warm blanket.

Many Pagans turn to nature for support as well. My friend Kathy told me that when her daughter was diagnosed with a life-threatening illness, she dealt with it like this: "I went out into the forest and played my Native American flute and tried to quiet myself and see if I could get any wisdom from the goddess." She added, "I have also found that if I can make myself do it, just simply lighting a candle and blessing the day and my troubles helps me calm and center, at least for a while."

This is a pretty typical Pagan reaction to crisis: turn to nature, the gods, and our own inner wisdom. And try to accept the difficult situation as a blessing in disguise, no matter how hard that might be to do.

....

Nature

Nature is a big part of how many Witches cope when things get rough. We go to the woods, as Kathy did, or sit by the water, whether it be ocean, lake, or stream. Many Pagans have some form of water in or around their homes to use for calming and meditation; fountains are a common fixture in the Witch's house and gardens.

We might walk outside at night and look at the full moon or count the many stars that shine overhead. This action has two purposes for most of us: it soothes our souls by helping us to feel connected to the great cosmos around us, and it can remind us of how small we are in the giant scheme of the universe, and that therefore our problems are pretty small, too.

Nature is often quiet and peaceful, and can bring that peace to our tattered spirits. It is also filled with affirmations of life. A bird's song can make you smile even during the most difficult of times. It can also remind you that beauty still exists, no matter how ugly the world around you might seem at times.

Sources of Wisdom

We talked about how Pagans often turn to the gods for support during times of crisis; the gods can also be a source of wisdom when we are trying to find our way through difficult times. In the midst of a chaotic and upsetting situation, often it is hard to see our way to a solution, even if it is right in front of us. But as Witches, we have a few extra options to call on when we need clarity or to decide between two or more courses of action.

We can, of course, simply stand at our altars or under a tree, and ask the gods to send us guidance. The trick here is to really listen for the answer. The gods do not always speak loudly, and their reply shows up, as often as not, as that quiet voice in our own hearts.

Witches also often turn to various means of divination in their search to find the best possible solution to a problem. Tarot cards and runes are traditional tools for finding answers to life's tricky challenges. Some folks can read for themselves and often turn to the cards or stones for guidance. Others find it more difficult to get clear answers when their own emotions are involved and seek out help from other Pagans with talent in those particular areas.

Magick and Ritual

Or you could do a spell.

There are many times when the best approach is a straightforward, mundane action. But there are often ways to incorporate ritual and spellwork to give your mundane solutions a helping hand. Just don't expect to do a spell and have it solve all your problems without any further effort from you; unfortunately, life rarely works that way. (Bummer.)

And don't limit yourself to thinking of ritual only in the context of magickal work. Ritual can be any ceremony or rite that is done for a specific purpose.

Witches often find comfort in the old ways of doing things, as in the way my circle-sister Chris dealt with the death of her beloved grandmother. When I asked her for an example of how being Pagan had helped her deal with a crisis, she told me this story:

> My sisters and I did the "Pagan" thing to say goodbye to my grandmother. We bathed her body and lotioned it with her favorite scent while talking to her spirit, which I could feel near in the room. We told her, while her body was still warm, that we loved her and that we would make sure her funeral was done correctly (something important to her).
>
> Then on the day of her interment, we stood and watched until the last shovel full of soil was placed over her casket. Gruesome? Maybe to some. But to us, it was in the old tradition where the only way that the deceased found their way to their final resting place was by being surrounded by those who loved them the most. The fact that I watched over all of that and made sure to fulfill my promises to my grandmother comforts me today.

This story is a good example of how connecting with the old ways and rituals of doing things can often bring us serenity during difficult times. As Witches, we tend to be drawn to the traditions of our ancestors, and sometimes we can use these traditions to ease our hearts and minds when life gets tough.

And there are many times when doing a magickal ritual or spell can help, too. We can do spells to ask the gods for help with whatever problem we are dealing with at the moment, or we can do a ritual to increase our ability to cope in general. It never hurts to ask for strength, patience, and good old-fashioned luck.

Here are two of my favorite spells for times of difficulty. The first one is from my book *Circle, Coven & Grove: A Year of Magickal Practice*. The second is one that I wrote a couple of years ago and have used a few times with good results. I hope that if you need to use them, they will bring you the help you need.

For both of these, a simple approach is probably best. Do them outside if possible, or in a darkened, quiet room. Light a few candles to create a peaceful atmosphere, and put a few drops of a calming oil in a defuser or on the candles themselves; lavender, bergamot, chamomile, lily of the valley, jasmine, orange, rose, and vanilla are among my favorites for this purpose.

You may want to start with a meditation or a positive affirmation, such as "I am calm and at peace," to put you in a better frame of mind for casting the spell, since it is hard to gather the necessary focus for effective spellwork when we are in the grip of powerful emotions.

It may also help to do a grounding and centering visualization. If you are standing, see yourself putting down roots deep into the earth through the base of your feet (if you are sitting, you can start from the base of your spine; both work equally well). Send the roots down deeper and deeper, as if you were a tree looking for nutrition and balance. Then send branches up into the sky through the upper part of your body, reaching for the light and clarity of the world above. When you feel yourself grounded and supported from above and below, open your eyes and light a white candle while saying one of the following spells:

Adjusting to Change Spell

In times of change, to ease transition
I call upon the goddess wise
To help me find my new position
Underneath her moonlit skies
Guide my spirit, hands, and heart
In this time of shifting tide
Aid me with the tasks I start
While easing what I lay aside
Whether grief or joyous birth
Sadness or release
With air and water, fire and earth
The goddess brings me peace

Spell to Ease Life's Path

I ask the gods my path to smooth

My psyche calm, my spirit sooth

Send me comfort through the day

As I walk the Blessing Way

Ease my way when money's needed

Ease the road to heart's desire

Ease the troubles life can bring us

With the power of air and fire

Ease the making of life's choices

Ease the deaths and ease the births

Ease the problems of the body

With the power of water and earth

Keep me wise and keep me happy

Keep me healthy night and day

Keep me strong and keep me grateful

As I walk the Blessing Way

When you are finished, be sure to take as long as you need to soak up the feeling of peace and balance. Envision your life calm and free of crisis. If you want, you can use a sage smudge stick or some incense to clear away any lingering remnants of negativity before you return to your everyday life.

Something to Think About:

What was the last big crisis that you had to deal with? How did you use your Pagan beliefs and practices to help you cope with it? Was there something you could have used that you didn't? Write it down and put it where you'll see it the next time your life gets crazy.

part three

the
outer
WITCH

Your Home Is Your Temple
The Pagan Household

They say that a man's home is his castle. If you are a Witch, then your home is your temple—literally.

Even if you are in a group and mostly celebrate full moons and holidays somewhere else, you probably have an altar set up somewhere in your house— if you're really lucky, maybe more than one. And all of us practice our Craft at home at least some of the time. For many, it is the center of their religious experience.

Many Witches have houses that are filled with decorations that reflect their spiritual beliefs and their connection to Pagan cultures from around the world. For some folks, that means wall hangings with Celtic designs and statues of Brigid. For others, it may be the Egyptian cat goddess Bast or miniature cauldrons filled with candles. Some Witches stick with one culture, while others have eclectic households full of colorful symbols from many Pagan belief systems.

There is no right or wrong way to integrate your Pagan beliefs into the place that you live. However, some Witches—those whose spaces are small or shared with others who do not believe as they do—can be challenged to create a home that truly feels like the temple it should be.

In this section of the book, we'll look at ways to create a spiritual foundation in the home that will support and enrich our everyday lives, regardless of the circumstances under which we live.

Something to Think About:

If you could pick only one item to symbolize your spiritual beliefs, what would it be—would it be a pentacle, a statue of a particular goddess, a representation of the Tree of Life? Why this particular symbol? What about it appeals to your Pagan soul?

Something to Try:

Make a list of your favorite Pagan symbols, goddesses and gods, and the elements of nature that appeal to you the most. See what traditional items you include and what you leave off because it doesn't happen to resonate with you.

Altars, Circles, and Other Places of Worship

Where and how a Witch choses to practice his or her Craft varies widely from Pagan to Pagan. Some folks like to be highly structured: a formal altar, a permanant stone circle set into the ground, or an elaborate room set aside only for spiritual concerns. Other people lack either the space, the privacy, or the inclination to be so ceremonial, and are just as happy to walk outside and stand under the full moon, or walk into the woods with nothing more than a simple cloak and an athame. There is no right place to practice Witchcraft; the right place for you is the one where you feel a connection to nature, the freedom to be yourself, and the presence of the gods.

Altars

My *Merriam-Webster's Collegiate Dictionary* defines an altar as a table that serves as a center of worship or ritual. Of course, this can mean different things to different people—especially if those people are Witches.

An altar can be natural or man-made, temporary or permanent, simple or complicated. As with any other element of your spiritual practice, it should suit your particular needs and reflect your own personality.

To give you an idea of what I'm talking about, let me tell you about the altars I use in and around my own home. Since I use more than one altar for more than one purpose, I pretty much cover all the possibilities I listed above. But many Pagans are content with just one, in which case you should create the altar space that resonates most strongly with your inner sense of what's right for you.

My primary altar is a wooden shelf that hangs on my bedroom wall. This is a fairly traditional permanent arrangement, with a pentacle carving hanging above, a cloth decorated with sparkling stars, candles for the goddess and god, containers of salt and water, incense, a few crystals, and the like.

This is where my athame lives when I'm not using it, and there is usually a piece of paper with a spell for whichever magickal goal I am working on at the moment, to remind me of my intention to send energy in that direction. Small objects may come and go, but the basic setup stays more or less the same.

This altar is private and rarely viewed by anyone other than me. It is also safely out of the reach of my cats, an important prerequisite for any permanent altar in my house.

I mostly use this space for solitary spellwork, although I often simply stand in front of it to talk to the gods or light a candle in thanks on occasions when I am feeling particularly grateful for their gifts. I rarely bother to go through formal circle casting or quarter invocations when I use this altar, although when actually casting a spell I might visualize myself surrounded by a protective white light.

The coven altar, on the other hand, is a completely different matter. My group, Blue Moon Circle, usually gets together on new moons, full moons, and sabbats, and we almost always gather at my house, which acts as the group's covenstead.

For group work, I have both an inside and an outside altar, the outside one being a simple rock slab that is permanently set into the ground in a circle behind the barn.

When we are forced inside by the weather (which happens a lot here in upstate New York), we use a wooden table that I had specially made for me by one of the artists at the shop I run. It's a round table with sides that fold down, so it can be put against a wall, out of the way, when it is not being used, and it is low enough that we can comfortably sit around it on cushions.

This altar is both temporary and permanent in that it is always used for this purpose, but it isn't kept set up at all times like the one in my bedroom.

Since this altar is used by the many Witches in my group and our invited guests, it has a very different energy than my personal altar. When in use, it is decorated with a cloth, quarter candles, etc., and we always cast a formal circle and invoke the quarters before inviting the gods to join us.

I have also been known to use whichever regular old table is handy and/or easily portable when leading rituals away from home. Since I perform weddings and handfastings, I often end up using a mundane table as an altar, since that's all that's available. It doesn't really make much difference in the end; it is the intention of the one who uses it that makes a table into an altar, not the table itself.

So how do you go about creating an altar for yourself if you don't already have one? Well, you could follow the directions available in the many "introduction to Witchcraft" books you probably have sitting on your bookshelf. Almost all of them will tell you what to put on an altar and how to put it there. (Now, wait—was that goddess candle on the left and god candle on the right, or vice versa?)

Or you could just listen to your heart and set up your altar in whatever way seems right to you. There is nothing wrong with following instructions out of a book; many of us start out that way. But if that doesn't appeal to you, or if you've been using that kind of altar and it no longer seems to work for you, here is another way to approach setting up your perfect space for worship and ritual.

Start with your list of favorite Pagan symbols, if you made one earlier, or take a moment now to reflect on what traditional altar items seem right for your own personal ritual space.

Think about what these items actually stand for, not just their obvious uses. For instance, incense often represents the elements of air and/or fire. If you live in a place where you can't burn incense, are allergic, or just plain don't like the stuff, you can substitute a feather for air or a drawing of a flame for fire. Don't be afraid to think outside the box. We are Witches, for goodness' sake; we are "outside the box" people!

If you already have an altar, you can keep the things that fit your new space and discard or put away the ones that don't. And remember that an altar is often a work in progress—you don't need to have everything that you'll eventually want to use on it in order to begin setting it up, and you'll almost certainly add things to it as time goes by.

Once you have everything you want for your altar, figure out the best space to put it in. What room feels like the most positive or safest place to practice your Craft? Do you need to keep it away from curious eyes, your children's fingers, or (like me) an overly curious animal friend? Try to pick a space where you will actually use it. It is all very well to tuck away your altar in the guest room upstairs, but if you never go in there, it won't do you much good. If you want to be more flexible, you could even set up an altar on a rolling table and move it wherever you want.

When you have a table or shelf set up in the room you've chosen, place the items you picked out on it in whichever way seems most appropriate. Feel free to move them around until they feel right. Then say a blessing and consecrate your wonderful new altar, the center for worship in the temple that is your home.

Circles

Most Witches conduct their ritual work inside a circle. This is a space that is consecrated for safe and effective magickal work, and like an altar, it can be either temporary or permanent.

My group often uses a permanent circle that I set up behind the barn at my house in the country. It is located close enough to the house that it is not terribly inconvenient to haul all of the ritual supplies out there, but it is far enough away to be safe from prying eyes. It is also an area that I don't need to use for anything else, which makes it perfect for a permanent sacred space.

This circle is neither complicated nor fancy. The perimeter of the circle is constructed of flat stones I dug out of the ground in various places around the property, laid out in the traditional nine-foot circle that many Witches prefer. Nine is a powerful magickal number, and a circle that is nine feet across is large enough to encompass quite a few people, yet small enough to use with only five or six. Still, there is no reason why you can't make your circle larger or smaller than this, depending on your needs.

Inside the stones, there is a fire pit and the large flat stone we use for an altar. That's it. Period. See, I told you it wasn't complicated. The truth is, a circle doesn't need much to be a magickal space. In most cases, simpler is probably better. A circle is more about the energy you bring into it than the space itself.

In the case of my outside circle, we use some of the flat stones around the edge of the circle to hold candles, or we place the quarter candles in stands that can be stuck into the ground. We use the fire pit for the rituals where it seems appropriate, and we put the usual supplies on the altar.

You might wonder why we even have a permanent circle, if that's all there is to it. The reason has to do with both intent and energy, like much else in Witchcraft. A circle that is used repeatedly for magick retains the essence of that magickal work and becomes more and more powerful over time. By dedicating that space to your practice of the Craft, it is also a way of saying to the universe that you are a Witch.

In truth, we have done so much magickal work both inside and outside my house, the entire place has become a kind of permanent sacred space. You can actually feel the difference over time, which is pretty amazing. You will find the same thing happening to your house, in any place where you have a circle that is used over and over.

Some Witches draw or paint permanent circles on the floor, then cover them with a rug when they are not being used. Others use some sort of cloth that can be spread out during ritual use, which is often painted with mystical symbols or has a large pentagram in the middle. Whether or not you create either a permanent or portable circle space will depend primarily on your living situation, though it might also reflect your preference for impromptu ritual versus a more organized style. Neither way is wrong, and many Witches practice for years with only the circle they create out of the energy of the rituals they perform.

Other Places of Worship

No discussion of Pagan worship is complete without talking about the ritual spaces that the gods themselves create—the natural sacred space of forest, meadow, beach, and garden. For many Witches, nature is the only altar they will ever need, and a ring of trees their only circle.

I have no argument with that. After all, that is the way our ancestors must have started out. For them, the gods were in the stars, the moon, the sun, and the sea. And in many ways, that is still true for us modern Pagans, although it may be harder for us to find that connection if we live in the midst of concrete buildings and paved roads.

No matter how many indoor altars or circles we have, it is important to remember to now and again leave the comfort of our homes and go out into the sacred space formed by nature. The most elaborate altar is no substitute for walking barefoot in the grass, wading in the water, or sitting under a tree and listening to the wind whisper through the branches.

For most Pagans, our places of worship are a combination of the mundane and the magickal, the ancient and the modern. So bring in a few pieces of the natural world to put on your inside altar, and don't forget to occasionally hug a tree.

Something to Try:

After you have created your altar or rearranged your old one, sit in front of it for a few moments with your eyes closed. Can you feel a change in the energy of that area? Try it again once you have used it a few times. Does it seem different now? Does it seem balanced and positive, or is something missing or out of place? How does your altar make you feel—safe? Blessed? If you have created a circle, can you tell when you have crossed outside its boundaries?

If there is a special place where you go outside that feels sacred to you, be sure to say thank you the next time you are there.

Sharing Your Space
with Non-Pagans

I live alone (well, if you can call anyone who lives with five cats alone). My home is mine to do with as I wish and decorate in any way I choose. I can hang up pentacles, collect dozens of crystals, and leave stacks of Witchcraft books out on every table in the place if I so desire.

But not everyone has this kind of freedom. In many cases, a Witch may share his or her space with someone else who is not a Pagan, whether that person is a parent, a roommate, or a significant other. Sometimes this isn't a problem. Other times, it is.

So what is the best way for a Witch to cope with living with a muggle? (The term for a non-Pagan is actually "cowen," in case you didn't know, but the word isn't used much anymore.) It depends on the situation.

There are various ways in which non-Pagans react to living with a Witch. These can range from enthusiastic support to horrified disapproval, with open-minded interest, willful ignorance, or benign disinterest falling somewhere in the middle. How much of your witchy self you choose to expose to the person or persons with whom you share your space will probably depend on which one of these attitudes you are dealing with on a daily basis.

Enthusiastic Support

Short of living with another Pagan, which few of us are lucky enough to do, this is the best scenario a Witch could hope to have. Enthusiastic support means that the person you live with, while not actually a Pagan, is completely open to your identity as a Witch. He or she encourages your spiritual practices and might even attend the occasional ritual or other Pagan event with you.

A couple of the women in my coven are lucky enough to be in this position. Their husbands support them wholeheartedly in their beliefs and easily accept the time and energy they devote to the group and to their individual practices. The guys don't come to new moon or full moon rituals, for the most part, since these are devoted to serious and often intense magickal work, but they are cheerful participants at all our sabbat celebrations. (I'm almost completely certain they are not coming just for the desserts.)

Both of these men are what I like to call "peripheral Pagans," in that their beliefs are not all that different from those of a practicing Witch, but they don't actively pursue a Pagan lifestyle.

If you are a Witch living with someone who provides you with enthusiastic support, you probably don't have to change your behavior too much from that of the Witch who lives alone. There may be fewer overt signs of your beliefs around the house, but you will undoubtedly be free to have an altar, and your books and magickal paraphernalia can be left out in plain sight. In short, you are a fortunate Witch.

Open-Minded Interest

If you can't have the enthusiastic support, open-minded interest isn't a bad second place. If you live with someone who views your Pagan lifestyle with open-minded interest, he or she probably doesn't share your beliefs in many ways, but is at least willing to let you live your life your way. Oftentimes, these folks will even go so far as to read a book or two on Witchcraft or go to a ritual once or twice, just to get a better idea of where you're coming from.

For teens, this is sometimes a parent who is open to their child following a different path but wants to check it out to make sure it isn't dangerous. If this is your situation, as much as you probably don't want your mother or father poking around in your personal business, it is almost always better to let them get a good enough look at what you're doing to be reassured.

After that, they'll probably leave it alone, though they might ask an occasional question. And if you are seriously interested in the Craft, instead of just doing it to be different or to piss people off, you'll no doubt welcome the opportunity to share your excitement and new knowledge.

As an adult, whether you are sharing your space with a roommate, a friend, or a significant other, life is definitely easier if they maintain an attitude of open-minded interest. I had a boyfriend back when I first started practicing the Craft who had no interest in attending ritual or studying Witchcraft in any depth. On the other hand, he did go to a lecture on Wicca given by my then-high priestess at a local Unitarian church, and he often talked with me about our different spiritual beliefs in an open and accepting way.

If you live with someone who is open-minded but truly has no Pagan leanings, you may want to use a little more restraint in your decorating than you might have if you lived by yourself. Try to keep the lines of communication open and discuss any new Pagan addition to the house to make sure that it doesn't seem like too much for the other person. While you don't necessarily want to compromise on your beliefs, you also don't want to push them on someone else.

If you are going to do a serious ritual or magickal working of any kind, you may want to do it at a time when the other person isn't home, or take the effort to let him or her know what you'll be doing and ask not to be interrupted for a while. Remember that a non-Pagan may not know enough not to touch your magickal tools or leave your altar space alone unless you let them know it's important.

Benign Disinterest

Benign disinterest means that someone doesn't care what you do but has no interest in being involved in any way. In this case, the person involved is probably happiest if they don't have to see or hear much that concerns your Pagan beliefs and practices, although he or she won't do anything to discourage you from following your own path.

This is often the case with people you are not that close to, like college roommates or housemates who are not good friends. Sometimes it can be the situation if you are married or otherwise involved with someone whose religious background is very different from yours.

One of my circle-mates is married to a man who was brought up with very traditional Christian beliefs. He doesn't truly understand her interest in Witchcraft (although she has been practicing for most of their married life, twenty years now), and much of it makes him uncomfortable. On the other hand, he loves her and wants her to be happy, so he doesn't stand in her way.

Mostly, he thinks her Pagan beliefs are kind of weird, but he accepts that they are part of who she is. Their house has very few overtly Pagan symbols on display, and they compromise over the sabbat celebrations by having him skip the ritual and come later to share the feast with all of us afterwards.

In some cases of benign disinterest, the other person will be perfectly open to you having a certain amount of Pagan influences around the home as long as it is not overwhelming. You can probably find a way to set aside a private space for a discreet altar and have the occasional goddess statue here and there. The Witchcraft books may be tucked in a corner, but they probably won't have to be hidden. Again, communication and compromise are the keys to happily sharing your space.

Willful Ignorance and Mockery

This is the person who, on the surface, pretends not to care about your "alternative" spiritual path. Most of us have met one or two like this: those who affect disinterest or even seem to be accepting of your religion but in reality clearly have a problem with it.

I went out with a guy like this for a while. He swore up and down that he didn't mind that I was a Pagan, even thought it was kind of cool. On the other hand, he was really uncomfortable when we got to the "talking about moving in together" stage when I mentioned that I would want to have a bunch of

Witches over from time to time. And after a while, the "so, are you roasting babies tonight?" cracks got a little old.

The truth was, he really wasn't comfortable with it at all. And he used jokes and mockery to cover it up so he could seem like he was.

Sometimes these folks don't want to admit to you that they disapprove, either because they are afraid of jeopardizing the relationship (whether that is family, friend, or romantic), or because they don't want to make a fuss and would rather pretend that everything is fine.

In other cases, these people may not even admit to themselves that they have a problem; after all, nobody wants to think of him- or herself as prejudiced or close-minded. So the mockery just slips out as an outward expression of their true inner feelings.

How you deal with willful ignorance and mockery will depend in part on how important the person is to you and how much time you have to spend with them. For instance, if it is a co-worker you rarely talk to, you will probably be better off just ignoring the behavior and feeling sorry for the person.

On the other hand, in the case of a serious relationship, you are probably better off trying to educate and enlighten your friend, lover, or family member and bringing the issue out into the open. At the very least, you can put your foot down about the snide comments, even if you can't change the person's opinion or discomfort level.

Horrified Disapproval

Unfortunately, if you are dealing with horrified disapproval, no amount of compromise or communication is likely to help you. If you have to cohabitate with people who think that Witches are evil and misguided, it is unlikely that you are going to be able to change their minds.

In some cases, you may have very little choice in the matter. If you are underage and still living at home or stuck with a disapproving college roommate, your best bet may be to keep as low a profile as possible, practice your Craft in private, away from prying eyes, and wait it out until you can move out and into a freer living situation.

Sadly, sometimes the only way to deal with horrified disapproval is to make a choice between your spiritual practice and the person who has a problem with your beliefs.

It is a well-known fact in the Pagan community that some marriages don't survive when one partner becomes involved in the Craft and the other doesn't. Like many other issues that can tear a relationship apart, this situation often indicates that there was a problem in the marriage to begin with, but that doesn't make it any easier for the Witch who is forced to choose between an open practice of his or her faith and a relationship that may still work in other ways.

Is it still possible to be a Witch if you live with someone who views all things Pagan with horrified disapproval? Of course it is. But in this case, like many of those who came before us, you must practice your Craft in the shadows and hide your beliefs behind closed doors. And in the long run, if your beliefs are important enough, you will probably reach a point where you will seek to share your life with those who will let you live openly as an Everyday Witch.

Something to Think About:

If you share your living space with one or more other people, which of these five categories do they fall into? Which of your actions make it easier for you to coexist? Is there anything that you do that makes it harder? If so, what can you do to change that without compromising your beliefs?

Housecleaning and Spiritual Cleansing

What does housecleaning have to do with being a Witch? More than you might think, actually.

You have probably heard that old saying that cleanliness is next to godliness. Well, in our case, we might say "goddessliness" if there were such a word, but the meaning is still the same. To put it simply: it is hard to be pure of spirit if you are living in a pigsty.

If your home is truly your temple, it only makes sense that you would want to treat it in a positive and respectful way. And while few of us are able to keep the places where we live spotless and neat all the time (especially if we share our space with kids, pets, or other such messy creatures), it is important to at least make the effort.

There are two different types of cleaning to consider: the mundane (regular old housecleaning) and the magickal (spiritual cleansing). Depending on how you go about it, you can often combine the two for even more effective results.

Housecleaning

I'm not a huge fan of housecleaning, to be honest, but I do enjoy the satisfaction I feel when I take a dirty or cluttered space and transform it into a clean and organized one. I also find that I get dragged down when surrounded by clutter and become less and less able to focus.

This makes sense when you think about it; as human beings, we are affected by our environment. The more sensitive you are to your environment, the more true this is—and let's face it, most Pagans tend to be pretty sensitive.

Still, housecleaning can feel like a fairly daunting task, and it often seems easier to live with an unpleasant mess than it is to force yourself to actually do something about it. But if you've hit the point where your dust bunnies are being eaten by dust cougars, you might want to consider some of the following suggestions for making housecleaning a little easier, healthier, and maybe even fun.

BREAK THE JOB DOWN INTO SMALLER PIECES—If you look at the big (messy) picture, it often seems overwhelming. Instead, make a list, and take one room at a time or one or two tasks each day.

ESTABLISH A ROUTINE—Once something is part of your daily schedule, it is easier to do. For example, every night I clean the litter boxes before I go to bed. It is not my favorite job, but by doing it every day, they never get too out of hand, and it has become such a part of my pre-bedtime ritual, I don't even think about it.

DO WHATEVER YOU CAN TO MAKE CLEANING FUN—I turn on my favorite music—*loud*—and bop around the house as I clean. (It is probably a good thing I live alone.) When one of my favorite songs comes on, I might even stop and dance for a few minutes before returning to my chores, energized and happy.

IF YOU LIVE WITH SOMEONE ELSE, CLEAN TOGETHER—You get more done in a shorter time, and you can even have contests to see who can get their tasks done more quickly.

WHENEVER POSSIBLE, USE NATURAL CLEANING PRODUCTS—They smell nicer, work just as well, and are easier on both your health and the health of the environment. (Many commercial cleansers are toxic to pets as well, so you would be doing yours a favor by avoiding them.) You can even make up many simple cleaning solutions using common house-hold items such as baking soda and vinegar. Since Witches are all about living in partnership with our Mother Earth, we probably don't want to use poisonous and nonbiodegradable products to clean our homes. And as a bonus, homemade cleaners are often much cheaper than the store-bought kind.

PRIORITIZE—If you can't keep every part of your home neat and tidy all the time (and few of us can—I'm begging you, do *not* look in my upstairs closets), figure out what is most important, and concentrate on that first. I try to make sure that my altar space stays neat out of respect, and that the four main spaces I use the most—bedroom, living room, kitchen, dining room (which doubles as my writing area)—are cleaned up at least once a week. The craft room upstairs, however, is usually only truly clean once or twice a year and can be something of a disaster area in between. Figure out which rooms are most important to keep under control: where do you need to be able to relax, or think clearly, or get together with friends? Where do you do your spiritual work, magickal work, or mind/body exercises like yoga? These spaces should be first on your list.

All of us go through periods of time when life gets away from us, and the housecleaning has to be allowed to slide for a bit. But try not to let it happen on a regular basis; remember that our goal is to be physically, mentally, emotion-ally, and psychically healthy, and it is hard to achieve this if you are surrounded by chaos. Chaos invites imbalance and can hide shadows and negativity that might otherwise be clear to us.

Besides, those dust cougars can be downright scary.

Spiritual Cleansing

Spiritual cleansing is different from housecleaning, but it serves the same basic purpose. While mundane housecleaning will clear and organize your physical surroundings, spiritual cleansing will do the same thing on an emotional and energetic level.

Just as our homes become cluttered and messy when we don't take the time to tend to them, so do the various elements of our spiritual life. It is a good idea to periodically make the effort to spiritually cleanse our bodies and our environments.

There are many different methods of doing this, and it isn't always necessary to do all the steps I list here. You can pick whichever techniques appeal to you and add in some of your own if you have them. And, of course, you can still play music if you want to, but for this particular kind of cleansing, something meditative like drumming or chanting might be a better choice than good old rock 'n' roll.

Note: before you start, you may want to go through the house and throw out or give away items you no longer use or anything that has negative memories or emotions attached to it.

Spiritual Spring Cleaning

INTENTION—Take a moment to focus on your intention of clearing away negativity and bringing in positive, cleansing energy. If the weather allows, open at least one window in every room.

SMUDGING—Light a sage smudge stick and walk from room to room with it. If you live in a place with more than one story, start at the bottom (the basement or first floor) and work your way up to the top. In each room, walk around in a clockwise (deosil) direction, wafting the sage as you go. Pay special attention to any place that energy can enter or leave, such as doorways, windows, and chimneys. As you leave each room, shut any open windows. When you finish with the last space, be sure to visualize your home as clear, open, and full of potential.

SALT AND WATER—If there is more than one person working on the cleansing, you can do this next step in conjunction with the smudging. For instance, whenever anyone in my circle moves into a new home, the entire group goes over and does a spiritual house-cleansing ritual together. If alone, do this step once you are finished with the sage, following the same pattern. Sea salt is probably best suited for this use, but regular table salt will do if that's all you have. Just as you did with the smudge stick, sprinkle salt and water (either separately or mixed together) around each room. To integrate an element of protection into your cleansing, you can even add a few drops of rosemary essential oil or soak some rosemary for a few days in the water you're going to use.

BLESSING—When you feel that you have gotten your space as free of negativity as possible, you can finish off the cleansing by saying a blessing over your home. You can write this yourself or use a favorite one from a book. Feel free to use this simple house-blessing charm:

> *Bless this home where I reside*
> *Keep it safe from woe and harm*
> *Watch over those who here abide*
> *I make it so by will and charm*

OPTIONAL EXTRAS—Here are a few other practices you can integrate with your regular cleaning routine to keep your home free of negativity and emotional clutter.

- When you mop your floors, add a few drops of some magickal purification and protection oils to the mop water. I like to use a combination of geranium, lemon, and rosemary.

- This works for sweeping, too; just sprinkle a few drops on your broom before you start and focus on your intention to sweep away negativity while you clean.

- If you have rugs, you can make a natural carpet freshener by adding cleansing or uplifting oils to baking soda. Just sprinkle it on the carpet, leave for a bit, and then vacuum as usual.

- The simplest recipe for a natural cleaner is to make a paste out of baking soda and water (with a little Borax mixed in if you need extra oomph to get out hard water stains or clean a particularly grungy area). It is easy to add a drop or two of essential oil to make this "green" cleanser a little more magickal (not to mention better smelling).

- If you make up a homemade window cleaner using lemon juice, bless the lemon ahead of time to give it an extra bit of spiritual oomph. (A basic recipe would be a mixture of equal amounts of water and white vinegar with a drop or two of dishwashing soap and some lemon juice.)

- Air fresheners that you buy in the store are made from nasty chemicals, most of which don't even smell that pleasant. Instead, try combining nine parts water, one part alcohol (I use vodka, believe it or not), and a few drops of whichever essential oils you prefer. If you need serenity, try using geranium and bergamot. If you want something more energizing, you could use grapefruit and rosemary. I actually have a spray that I use in the shower every morning to help me wake up that combines those two oils and peppermint. Not only do they perk me up (and make my stinky well water smell better), but when used with magical intentions, they also add a bit of protection, purification, and a mental boost to each shower. What a great way to start out the day!

- Many essential oils come from herbs that are used magickally for protection. It is interesting to learn that these same oils often have "real-life" protective capabilities, because they are antiseptic, antibacterial, antifungal, antiviral, or even all of these at once. In short, they kill germs while they are clearing away negative energy. Oils that have these qualities that are also considered magickally protective include cinnamon, clove (which specifically is used to drive away negative forces), lavender, and lime. Any of these oils added to either a homemade cleaner or a "green" store-bought one can be used to add a protective boost to your house-cleaning efforts. (And remember that physical clutter attracts spiritual clutter and can open up your home to negative entities and energies. If you are a collector of stuff, you may want to consider lightening your load and/or doing some extra protection work when you clean.)

I'm sure you can think of plenty of other ways to combine the magickal techniques you already know with the mundane cleaning tasks you do on a regular basis. As with all of the other activities you do as an Everyday Witch, it is the extra focus and intention that you bring to each activity that makes it powerful and effective.

Something to Try:

Create a homemade cleaning solution using simple, safe, and natural ingredients. Add a drop or two of any magickal essential oil that is used for cleansing or protection, preferably one whose smell you like. If you want to, consecrate the cleaning solution so that it will automatically add a touch of spiritual cleansing whenever you do your mundane housework.

Here is a list of some of the best essential oils to use when cleaning and their corresponding magickal uses. Most of this information came from two different Scott Cunningham books: *Cunningham's Encyclopedia of Magical Herbs* (Llewellyn, 1985) and *Magical Herbalism* (Llewellyn, 1982). He also wrote a very useful book with David Harrington called *The Magical Household: Empower Your Home with Love, Protection, Health, and Happiness* (Llewellyn, 1983), which you might find useful as well.

CINNAMON—Protection, healing, and passion (you can use this one in the bedroom if you need to spice things up a bit).

CLOVE—Drive away negative forces, protect babies, aid memory, and attract the opposite sex (hmmm…at this rate, the bedroom may end up being the cleanest room in the house).

EUCALYPTUS—Healing (this is a great one to add to a room spray when someone is ill, and be sure to use it to clean up when someone has a cold, as this is another oil with antiseptic properties).

GERANIUM—Protection, healing, and love (an uplifting fragrance, this is a good one to use to cleanse a room after an argument or disagreement…or maybe before your in-laws come to visit).

LAVENDER—Protection, purification, and love (one of my favorites, it is also calming, so is good to use after a stressful day).

LEMON—Purification, love, and friendship (this oil will not only clean your house and leave it smelling good, it will help to make it a warm and welcoming place, and Cunningham recommends it for clearing away negative energy from magical tools and jewelry…especially anything you got second-hand).

LIME—Protection, love, and healing (a great room spray combines a number of different citrus oils for extra oomph).

ORANGE—Love (for those who really love to clean, there are a number of orange-based natural cleaners available).

PEPPERMINT—Protection (interestingly, this oil will also protect you from ants and other creepy-crawly things if you sprinkle or spray it around your kitchen).

ROSEMARY—Protection, purification, love, and mental sharpness (this is one of the best protective oils around and one of my personal favorites).

THYME—Purification (another oil that is antiviral, antibiotic, and antiseptic…but very powerful, so use sparingly).

....

Hint: A good source for information and recipes for "greener" and safer housecleaning alternatives is the book *Organic Housekeeping* by Ellen Sandbeck (New York: Scribner, 2006). And a great book on essential oils and their various medicinal and practical uses is *The Complete Book of Essential Oils & Aromatherapy* by Valerie Ann Worwood. This book is my essential oil bible, and I don't know what I'd do without it.

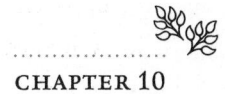

When You're Still in the Broom Closet

Setting Up Undercover Pagan Space

If you're one of the unlucky Witches who isn't free to come out of the broom closet just yet or you are currently living with intolerant others, don't assume that means you can't have an altar or practice your Craft in any way. With a little bit of ingenuity, you can create an undercover Pagan space for yourself and follow your heart with no one the wiser.

We talked in chapter two about the importance of symbols, and this is a perfect example of how we can use one thing to stand in for another without losing any of the power or significance attached to the original article. In this case, we will be substituting an innocuous everyday item for a more obviously witchy one.

Although it is traditional to set up an altar and enact rituals with particular witchy tools such as the four quarter candles, an athame, a chalice or cauldron, and a pentacle and the like, it is easy enough to find replacements that can easily be mistaken for just another part of the decor. Consider, for example, the popularity of moons, stars, suns, and faeries. Plenty of non-Pagans have these symbols around.

You could certainly hang a decorative ornamental broom on the wall. If you happen to have a picture of a Greek statue of a goddess, well, it just shows that you have good taste. And most people couldn't tell the difference between a statue of Bast and any other cute cat decoration. In many cases, the only thing that makes an object Pagan rather than mundane is your intent and the use to which you put it.

But suppose you want to have an actual altar setup but you don't want to use those traditional tools of Witchcraft because, grouped together, they are too obvious. Here are some suggestions for substitutes from my book *Everyday Witch A to Z*:

- God/goddess statues—gold/silver candles or a plaque of the Tree of Life (you could also use pictures of classical gods and goddesses, as we discussed above)
- Athame—fancy letter opener or wooden branch
- Chalice—any nice cup, goblet, or small bowl
- Salt and water—a stone and a seashell
- Quarter candles—a rock (earth), a feather (air), a shell (water), a tealight candle (fire)

Here are some additional suggestions:

- Instead of a cauldron, you could use a bowl filled with stones or sand.
- Any plant or plants could stand in for the god and goddess, and if you wanted you could research which ones are connected with a particular deity you follow. You could use two stones, such as moonstone for the goddess and tiger's-eye for the god. Or you could also hang a picture of the planet Earth to represent Gaia.
- To symbolize the four elements, you could use statues or pictures of animals—an elephant or tortoise (earth), dolphin or fish (water), raven or hawk (air), and a dragon or a salamander (fire).

Really, the only limit you have is how far you want to stretch your imagination. Witches hid their identities for centuries by disguising their magick in everyday activities that took place in kitchens, gardens, and sewing rooms.

If all else fails, a locked trunk or box will keep your witchy treasures safe from prying eyes, and you can always just stand outside under a full moon and bask in the presence of the goddess—a communion that no one can control or take away from you. It is important to keep in mind that inside your head, you can worship any way you choose; no tools are needed. Will, intent, belief, and love—where these things are, so are the gods.

Something to Try:

Make a list of all the "traditional" Pagan items you have on your altar or would want to have in a perfect world. Then come up with as many undercover substitutes as you can. You never know— maybe you will end up with something even better than your original list.

part four

the
social
WITCH

The Witch and Family

Where Do We Come From and Where Are We Going?

Our history as Witches is important to us, but no less important is our history as individuals. Who we are today is built on who we were yesterday, and the day before that, and the year before that. We wouldn't have gotten to this point without all the experiences that went into making us who we are—and our families are a big part of that.

For better or for worse, whether you had a happy childhood or a dysfunctional one, part of who we are as adults comes from who we were as children. And believe it or not, much of who we are as Witches comes from the religious and spiritual backgrounds we grew up with.

Sometimes we become Witches because our upbringings lacked so much of what we needed and were looking for in our lives. Sometimes we become Witches in addition to what we learned as we grew; there are plenty of Pagans who integrate the pieces of the religions they grew up in with the religion they follow now. Neither path is right or wrong; it is merely a matter of what works for each individual.

None of us exists in a vacuum. Our pasts help to create our futures, and the other people who are part of our lives help to create who we are as individuals.

In some ways, we are all works in progress, and those who surround us in our daily lives all help to paint part of the picture.

Who are the important people in your life, and what do they contribute to the creation of that work of art that is you? How do your interactions with others help to sculpt you—body, heart, and soul?

And what do you give back to them in return?

We all interact with others during the course of our days (and nights, if we're lucky). How do those interactions shape who you are as a person and as an Everyday Witch?

Something to Think About:

If you had to list the top five people in your life, who would they be? How much influence do they have on your daily activities? Are they family? Closer than family? How do they affect your spiritual life—do they make you stronger or cause you pain? What could you do to make your relationship with these five people better?

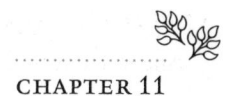

Sex and the Single Witch

Most traditional religions tend to have a lot of rules about sex. It may be looked upon as dirty or even sinful. Sex is allowed only in the context of marriage, and in the strictest sects, only when used for procreation. It is not acceptable to have sex without marriage, and there are strict taboos against sex with someone of the same gender, sex with more than one person, or even sex with yourself.

And they wonder why people are leaving these religions in droves.

Pagans, on the other hand, generally view sex as simply another facet of the human experience, neither good nor bad in and of itself. It can be a source of joy and communion, just plain fun, used to fuel a spell, or even as a form of worship. In short, like many of the other elements that make up the life of an Everyday Witch, sex is pretty much what you make of it.

So that means that the single Witch can go around having sex with anyone they fancy, all the time, regardless of the circumstances, right? Well, sorry, no. It doesn't exactly work that way, no matter what some other people might think. (See traditional religions, above.)

In truth, sex and love need to be approached carefully because they are so powerful and have the potential to cause as much pain as they do joy. Just like all the other important aspects of our lives, we need to keep in mind the seven basic Pagan beliefs (discussed in chapter two) when making decisions as single Witches.

Harm None

Obviously, this is the most important belief to keep in mind when dealing with the issues of sex and love. As Witches, we don't have rules that forbid any particular kind of sex; lesbian, gay, bisexual, and polyamorous (more than one lover) are all as acceptable as the more traditional one man/one woman pairing. Love is welcome in all of its many glorious colors, shapes, and sizes.

What isn't acceptable is using or abusing another person in the pursuit of sex or love. (Well, unless they happen to like being abused. But that's a whole other issue, and we're not going there.) So if you choose to have sex, you need to be as certain as you possibly can that no one is going to get hurt in the process—not even you.

Obviously, people can and do get carried away in the heat of the moment, but if you are still at the "thinking about it" stage, it's probably not a bad idea to consider the answers to a few simple questions. And if your answers make it look like you or anyone else will be sorry later, you might want to think again.

WHY ARE YOU HAVING SEX? The answers to this one might seem obvious: because it feels good and it's fun, or to express love and affection for your partner. But in reality, people have sex for lots of reasons that have little to do with simple passion. Are you having sex because you're drunk or stoned and not thinking straight? Are you angry and trying to get back at someone else or trying to prove that you are old enough, attractive enough, or powerful enough to get someone to sleep with you? As you can see, there are many motivations for sex that are neither fun nor healthy; try to take a clear, honest look at yours, and make sure that you are not doing it for all the wrong reasons.

ARE YOU AND YOUR PARTNER BOTH EQUALLY WILLING? This can be a tough one. Obviously, if your partner is saying no, then you need to stop and take a cold shower instead, or watch a movie, take a walk—whatever. But what if the person you are with is going along with sex because they feel pressured, either by you, by others, or even by themselves? Maybe they are trying to make you happy or are concerned that you will no longer want to be with them if they say no. Do your best to make sure that your partner is not just willing but honestly enthusiastic about the idea of sex. If they're not, you might want to discuss the subject openly and without pressure before moving on to the next step.

ARE BOTH YOU AND YOUR PARTNER CAPABLE OF MAKING A WISE DECISION ABOUT SEX? Hormones are powerful little critters. They race around to various parts of the body, stealing the blood we'd normally use to run our brains. It can be pretty hard to think clearly once the arousal process has started, but certain circumstances make it even more difficult and may lead to bad decisions that cause pain later on. Youth and inexperience, in particular, coupled with those powerfully raging hormones, have led many young Witches to leap when they might have been better off moving at a slow crawl. If you are underage, or your partner is underage, you may want to proceed with extra caution. Additionally, drugs and alcohol can lower inhibitions and interfere with rational thought; it is probably not a great idea to jump into bed (especially with a stranger) if you're not sure you're thinking clearly or you can't be sure of having safe sex.

IS THERE ANYONE ELSE INVOLVED WHO COULD GET HURT? If either you or your partner is married or seriously involved with someone else, there is almost a 100 percent chance that you will be causing harm. With the exception of mutually agreed-upon polyamorous relationships, there is no way to have sex with someone who is committed elsewhere without breaking the "harm none" rule. Even if the other person never finds out, you are still causing harm. If one or both of you is in an unhappy relationship with someone else, it is always better to resolve that issue and end one relationship before starting another one with someone else. And if you have children, you should probably be sure you are not exposing them to something (or someone) that could upset or frighten them. (For instance, if you want to have wild monkey sex on furniture all over the house, you might want to borrow somebody else's house or wait until the kids are off doing something elsewhere. Just a thought.)

······································

The Law of Returns

When dealing with sex and love, you want to remember that what you put out is what you will get back. If you are approaching the situation and your partner with honesty, affection, and compassion, then you're probably fine. On the other hand, if you are lying, manipulating, using, or in any way taking advantage of another person (even when they are knowingly allowing you to do so, as is the case in many abusive relationships), well, all I can say is "Duck." Sooner or later, the negative aspects of your dealings with others will come back to bite you, if only because that is often the gods' way of teaching us the error of our ways. Don't say I didn't tell you so.

······································

Personal Responsibility and Free Will

This is one of the trickiest areas of sex and relationships to balance out in a healthy and positive way. On the one hand, you have to be responsible for your own actions. On the other hand, you need to allow whoever you are involved with (whether on a temporary or a permanent basis) to exercise free will and make their own decisions. Which means that, theoretically, you can't influence them in ways that will interfere with their free will.

As anyone who has ever been in a relationship will tell you, it is pretty much impossible to interact with someone else, especially in the long term, without having an impact on the decisions they make and how and why they make them. It is the nature of human beings to react to each other, after all.

So all I can suggest is that you strive to maintain a healthy balance, with no one person in the relationship making the majority of the important decisions or always getting everything that they want, with the other person rarely getting what he or she needs.

Since we are talking about free will, what about love spells? This is an area in which many Witches find themselves in disagreement. Some folks say that it is impossible to cast a love spell without interfering with someone else's free will in some way. Others think that there is nothing wrong with casting a spell to make someone fall in love with you; after all, love spells are some of the oldest magick that there is.

For what it's worth, here is what I think: love spells are tricky, and it is easy to get them wrong, interfering with free will even when you don't intend to and opening yourself to long-lasting repercussions. What can I say—been there, done that, wrote the theme song.

Certainly it is possible to cast a love spell and have it work; there are plenty of Witches who will tell you that they found their true love through magick. But for everyone who has succeeded, there are a number who failed and made a giant mess in the process.

In my opinion, you are better off doing a spell to open yourself to love. That way, the only person you will affect is yourself. If you do choose to cast a love spell, try to do it in such a way that it will leave the choice up to the universe. Never cast a spell naming a particular person, since that will most assuredly cross the line into interfering with free will. Instead, ask the gods to send you the person who will be your most perfect match and for whom you will be the same.

Better yet, save the spells for prosperity and health, and let love find you whenever and wherever it will.

Words Have Power

When dealing with others in tender affairs of the heart (or other, less delicate body parts), remember that people are particularly vulnerable to the power of words when sex and love are involved. For many of us, it is impossible to separate our sense of self-worth from our sexuality. Rejection or acceptance should both be handled with equal delicacy, and special care should be taken when ending a relationship. Keep in mind that your words during the intricate mating dance that we call "relationships" can have repercussions long after you are gone.

How many of us have gone into new relationships with the words of our last lover still echoing in our heads? Careless statements uttered in anger can linger on and cause harm you never intended. Even kind words, like "I love you," can create problems when they are used to manipulate or influence someone. Of all the phrases in the language, this one may have the most power. Try not to use it unless you truly mean it. And if you mean it, say it often. Most of us go through life without hearing it nearly enough.

In general, be extra careful with your words when sex and love are involved—people's hearts are fragile and easily broken. Take care not to cause harm where none was intended, and treat others the way you would wish to be treated.

Magick Is Real

Can you use sex as a part of magick? Yes, you can, but this is not something to be done lightly. The Great Rite is a term for a ritual in which two people (usually, but not always, a male and a female) join themselves and their energies in a union that represents that of the god and goddess, or the male and female energies of the universe. This can be done to raise energy for a magickal task or simply to celebrate the gods in their glory.

These days, the Great Rite is mostly symbolic, enacted by placing an athame into a chalice (with the athame representing the male sex organ and the chalice the womb of the goddess). In some traditional paths, the high priest and high priestess of a coven may enact the Great Rite, but these days that is more likely to happen in a private ritual than in a circle full of other Witches.

If you decide that you want to work sex magick, the same rules apply as for normal sex, only more so. Be certain that both parties are not only willing but enthusiastic and that you are doing it for the right reasons. After all, if sex and love are powerful forces outside a magickal circle, think how powerful they will be inside one.

We Are Part of Nature

Our connection with nature is part of why we as Pagans tend to view sex quite differently than other religions. After all, as Cole Porter observed: birds do it, bees do it, even monkeys in the trees do it…

At its most basic, sex is simply another bodily function, designed to reproduce the species and cause pleasure. Just make sure you don't accidentally do one while pursuing the other. If you are fortunate enough to have someone with whom you can share this most natural of activities, and you are both (or all three, or whatever) willing, healthy, and unattached, then by all means, have at it.

Just keep in mind a few basics of nature that apply to Pagans as much as to anybody else, and do it safely. After all, sexually transmitted diseases don't care what religion you are or if you happen to be worshipping a goddess at the time. And unintended pregnancy can still mess up your life, even if you don't believe it's a sin.

So if you are going to have sex, make love, or otherwise dance the horizontal mambo, remember that nature is powerful, unpredictable, and can kick your life plans out the window faster than you can say "your place or mine?" Always be safe while you worship at the temple of sensual pleasures.

The Divine Is in Everything

One of our most important beliefs as Pagans is that each of us is, in essence, a little piece of God/dess. We are divine, and the divine is in all of us. So remember to treat yourself and your partner(s) with the respect that you would give to a deity. The Wiccan poem *The Charge of the Goddess* says, in part, "For behold: all acts of love and pleasure are my rituals." Each act of love is a communion with each other and with the gods, and should be enacted with awareness, joy, and care for all those involved.

If you feel the need to cast a love spell, here's one that should be safe but effective. Remember that it isn't always the right time for you or that the right person may not be available. Try putting the intent out into the universe, then enjoy all the other blessings in your life while you wait for things to fall into place in the love department.

Inside your sacred space, burn an incense that is associated with love magick—something like rose, lavender, or orange blossom would work well for this spell. If you like, you can invoke a god/dess who specializes in matters of the heart, such as Aphrodite or Venus, Astarte, Diana, Freya, Hathor, Hera, Inanna, Isis, Kwan Yin, Adonis, Cupid, Eros, Hymen, Krishna, or Vishnu.

Once your circle is cast, spend some time thinking about what kind of love you are looking for, and—more importantly—what you are willing to give of yourself to get it. Be realistic, be specific, but try to keep an open mind at the same time. (Hey, I didn't say it was easy, did I?)

For instance, you may want to focus on general traits, like patience or dependability, rather than superficial qualities, like height or hair color. You can even prepare a list ahead of time of the qualities you are looking for in a lover and what you are hoping to get out of a relationship.

Light a pink candle (or red, if you are looking for something passionate). Gaze at the candle for a while, then close your eyes and visualize that light surrounding your heart. See the light washing away any negativity left from past failed relationships, since those old feelings may stand in the way of your moving forward into a new, more successful interaction. Feel your heart open wide. (Be sure that you are in a safe and protected space before doing this!) Then recite the following spell:

Spell to Open Up to Love

I ask the moon and stars above
To open my heart to perfect love
Striving not, nor chasing after
But open wide to love and laughter

Hopeful am I and willing, too
To open myself to lover's woo
But while I wait for love that's meant
With myself I'll be content

I wish for love that's true and right
Filled with joy and shining light
I release all that which blocks my way
And open my heart to one who'll stay

Don't forget to follow this up with an occasional check-in to make sure that your heart is staying open. One good way to do this is to periodically (once a week or so) stand in front of your altar or bathroom mirror and mentally scan your heart for any signs of returning negativity or obstructions. You can say the spell once a month, if you feel it is necessary.

Something to Think About:

If you are sexually active, look at the list of reasons for having sex and ask yourself honestly what your reasons are and if there are any reasons that are less than healthy and positive.

Something to Try:

If you are in a relationship and sexually active, try putting aside a time to purposely make love as if you were worshipping a goddess or god with your body. Is this experience different from the way you usually connect with your partner? Are there parts of it that you liked enough to integrate them into future lovemaking?

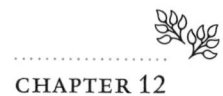
The Witch and Marriage

When most folks think about Witches and marriage, Samantha from the TV show *Bewitched* is probably the first example that comes to mind. Samantha, a Witch with amazing powers and an eccentric magickal family, was married to Darrin, an ordinary mortal. Most of the show revolved around poor, beleaguered Darrin's attempts to deal with his wife's exotic abilities, wacky family, and his own frustrations with both.

This doesn't exactly sound like a marriage made in heaven, but as those of you who are familiar with the show can attest, their relationship—despite the ups and downs and their many differences—was a strong one, based on a love that always ended up surmounting whatever difficulties their marriage encountered.

Let that be a lesson to us all.

Here in the real world, most of us can't wiggle our noses and make things fly across the room (although if you can, I'd love to see it), and your family might be odd, but they are unlikely to turn your husband into a toad.

Still, the challenges of trying to mesh differing belief systems, complicated by the fact that the practice of Witchcraft is still commonly misunderstood, can cause problems in even the most loving marriage. Even marriage to a fellow Pagan can have an issue or two that might not arise in a more conventional marriage—especially if you have different views of what is acceptable in the areas of sex and/or magick.

Does that mean that Witches can't have happy, successful marriages or long-term committed relationships? Of course not. But it may mean that we have to try a little bit harder, compromise a little bit more, or search a little longer to find someone who can accept and live with our Pagan lifestyle.

Before we get into the specifics of how to have a successful Pagan marriage, let's take a moment to define the term.

"Marriage" doesn't always mean the same thing to Pagans as it does to everyone else. For one thing, we Witches have our own type of wedding ceremony, called a handfasting. Some Pagan/Wiccan high priestesses and high priests who perform handfastings are also ordained ministers (at least on paper) so that the ceremonies they perform are legal and binding in the eyes of the state.

But not every Pagan couple feels the need or the desire to go the "proper" route just to satisfy society's rules. To their way of thinking, a handfasting ritual marries them in the eyes of their gods and their community, and that's all that matters. To complicate the issue, couples who get handfasted may choose to make a commitment for life or only for a year and a day.

Add to this the many Pagan couples who are in relationships that cannot legally be considered marriages under most current systems of government. (Boo, hiss.) As a high priestess, I happily performed a handfasting ceremony for two women. Does this count as a marriage? It did to them, to me, and to their families who came to witness the event.

So what do I mean when I talk about Pagans and marriage in this chapter?

For the sake of clarity, let's just say that I'm using that word to describe any long-term committed relationship between two people (or more, in a few cases) who have the intention to stay together for the foreseeable future.

In chapter eight, we talked about some of the conditions under which Pagans share their space with others: enthusiastic support, open-minded interest, benign disinterest, willful ignorance and mockery, and horrified disapproval. Married Witches usually end up dealing with at least one of these attitudes, and sometimes more than one if a partner approves but family doesn't, for example.

In a best-case scenario, a Witch will find and fall in love with another Pagan, which simplifies things greatly. (Although it certainly doesn't guarantee that things will go smoothly or that you won't end up coping with family members who disapprove of you both.)

Even in a marriage between two Pagans, issues will arise that require those involved to pay special attention to how they apply their spiritual beliefs to their everyday lives. For those whose path has led them to a non-Pagan partner, the challenges of marriage may be more complicated. On the other hand, opposites do attract, and differences can add spice and interest to a relationship.

The keys to a successful marriage, whether between two Witches or a Witch and a muggle, are four basic elements: commitment, communication, compromise, and compassion. You can think of these elements as the four watchtowers of marriage. Commitment is earth, communication is air, compromise is water, and compassion is fire.

Commitment/Earth

The element that takes a basic relationship and turns it into a marriage is commitment. Whether or not there is a formal ceremony—and it is possible for two people to simply stand together in a meadow and state their intentions to each other—commitment means that those involved have bound themselves together physically, emotionally, and spiritually.

Whether that binding is done symbolically—as is often the case in Pagan handfasting ceremonies when the couple's hands are tied together using ribbon or cord—or verbally, this act forges a powerful connection between the people involved.

Handfastings and weddings are rituals, after all. And the rule "As above, so below" means that vows made during ritual are binding on levels that go far beyond their obvious legal and social ramifications. As Witches, we know that marriage is not a commitment to be entered into lightly, since we are not only binding ourselves on a mundane level but on a magickal one as well.

On the other hand, once you have made that commitment, you can tap into that spiritual energy to help you keep your marriage on track. When things get difficult, it is a good idea to take a moment to remember those vows and how you felt when you made them.

If you can, sit together with some reminders of the ceremony you used (if there was one). Touch your handfasting cord, look at pictures, or just hold hands. Close your eyes and visualize that day when you stood as one and made a promise to each other. Remember how it felt to be that much in love, and allow that feeling to rise to the surface again.

If you are too angry to do this together, try taking a break and doing it separately. If you are fighting or at an impasse over some important issue, let go of the feelings of anger and frustration for a minute and allow yourself to focus on the love that brought you together and the commitment you made to work together as a couple.

Once you have done this, you may find that you can come together again and address your problems with clear minds and open hearts.

All relationships have their ups and downs, and it is rare for any couple to agree about everything all the time. But if you honor your commitment to the relationship and to each other, this earth element can provide a solid base on which to build a marriage that will last through the years.

Communication/Air

After love itself, communication may be the single most important element in a successful marriage. The couple that talks to each other—openly, honestly, and often—is much more likely to stay together than a couple that allows secrets, lies, or unspoken resentment to build until they reach critical mass and explode.

We talked in chapter three about the power of words; in a relationship, it is especially important to keep this rule in mind. Words, once spoken, can never be taken back. And words spoken in anger may cause wounds that may never heal.

On the other hand, words like "I love you," "I believe in you," "You are beautiful/fantastic/sexy," and "I am so happy to be with you" can bring light to even the darkest of days. And let's not forget a few of the other phrases that hold particular power, like "I'm sorry," "I'm listening," "I understand," and even "Please" and "Thank you."

Personally, I'm a big believer in total honesty in relationships. Now this doesn't mean you have to say things like, "Wow, honey, your butt looks huge in that outfit" (try "You always look beautiful to me" instead). But trust is the cornerstone to any marriage, and even the smallest lies can chip away at this foundation. The big lies can crumble it and turn it into dust.

Open communication can often keep small problems from becoming big ones. It is a good idea to set aside a time every day to check in with each other and discuss whatever is going on at the moment—at work, with family, personally, and as a couple. Many folks do this at dinner, but you can always talk before bed, during a nightly walk, or any other time that works for you both. The important thing is to keep the lines of communication open.

In many marriages, one person is a talker and one isn't. This means that the one who doesn't talk easily about feelings or himself/herself needs to make a special effort to communicate. And the one who does talk needs to be sure to listen. If issues arise, it is always better to tackle them while they are still small, rather than waiting until they are so immense that you can't discuss them without anger or resentment.

Watch your words and use them wisely, to build up rather than to tear down. Be honest and open with each other, and this air element will blow away the problems that might otherwise have built up into a tornado of trouble.

Compromise/Water

Marriage is all about going with the flow. Sometimes one of you gets your way, sometimes the other. You will each have good days and bad, and both partners will bring their own individual strengths and weaknesses into the relationship. The tricky part is finding a balance that works equally well for both of you, most of the time.

This is where compromise comes in. We all want to have things our own way; it is the nature of being human. But as adults, we realize that sometimes we have to give up one thing in order to have another. That's the basis of compromise. When the issue is small, like what to have for dinner, it is often easy to give in and let your partner make the decision.

But what about when the issue is more important: where to live, whether or not to have children, how to handle finances or family problems? Then compromise is tougher and even more important.

In a marriage where one partner makes most of the crucial decisions and gets his or her way on the majority of issues, the balance of power is out of equilibrium. Over the long term, this almost always leads to the "weaker" partner feeling unhappy, vulnerable, and inadequate. No marriage can be healthy and satisfying under these conditions.

Marriage is intended to be a partnership of equals. This means that important decisions all have to be made together and discussed until you can both decide on a course of action you can agree on. This often involves compromise, where the person who feels the strongest about one particular option may get part of what he or she wants but not all of it, or there is a trade-off in which each person gives a little bit, and you meet in the middle.

For instance, suppose that one of you really wants to live in the country, but the other one doesn't want to stop seeing friends who live in the city an hour away from your new home. A compromise might be to move anyway but promise to make trips back to see the friends often or invite them to visit periodically.

Communication and compromise are intrinsically tied together, since it is impossible to arrive at a compromise without serious discussion (or often a number of discussions). But if each of you is willing to occasionally give up something that is important to you so that the other partner can have what is important to them, and you make sure that both of you have an equal say in important decisions, compromise can go a long way toward building a strong and successful marriage.

But what about the issues on which there is no compromise—if, for instance, one of you wants children and the other does not. Sadly, if these are big-enough issues or if they happen often enough, you may have to face the fact that your relationship may not be workable.

Thankfully, most of the time this is not the case, and the Witch who is willing to compromise can usually keep a marriage flowing well and happily with the help of this water element.

Compassion/Fire

No marriage is complete without the fire element of passion. But this roaring flame has its softer, quieter side too: the element of compassion.

Compassion is the ability to look at the world through your partner's eyes and feel what he or she feels. Even more, it is taking the time and energy to feel with them, so that their pain is your pain, their fear is your fear, their concerns are your concerns. It is difficult to maintain anger or resentment in the face of true compassion, and this element can save you a lot of unnecessary stress and arguments if you both use it willingly.

Compassion isn't necessarily the same thing as agreement; you can disagree with someone yet still make an effort to understand their point of view. It has more to do with maintaining an attitude of open-minded acceptance, what the Buddhists call "loving kindness," even when the two of you are not on the same page.

Try to remember that all of us have our own particular needs, weaknesses, and things that push our buttons; if you can deal with each other's "stuff" compassionately and without taking it personally, I guarantee that your relationship will go a lot more smoothly.

The Christians (yeah, *those* guys) have a phrase that sums up compassion well: Do unto others as you would have them do unto you. If you treat your partner the way that you would like to be treated—with love, courtesy, and consideration—this gentle fire element will help to keep you both warm through even the coldest nights.

If you've hit a rough patch or just want to avoid one, you can try doing the spell that follows. If you are both Pagans, you can do it together, but it is fine to do on your own—there is nothing here to interfere with free will.

In sacred space, sit in front of two white or pink candles. If you want, place a vase of fresh roses or carnations on your altar. Play quiet, romantic music in the background. Take a few deep breaths, then close your eyes and think about all the aspects of the relationship that you value and appreciate. If you are doing this together, you can hold hands at this point.

Envision yourself surrounded by a shining white light, symbolizing the love of the gods. Take that love into your mind and your heart, and feel yourself expanding with feelings of love, patience, and acceptance.

When you are ready, open your eyes and light the candles (if doing this together, you can each light one or light a third, larger candle together and use it to light each of the smaller individual candles), then recite the following spell:

Spell for a Healthy Relationship

I call upon the elements' might
Fire and water, earth and air
To help me act with love and light
And walk the path that lovers share

Send compassion to my heart
Fire's warmth to light my way
As commitment was the start
The strength of earth is here to stay

Let compromise come easily
Like water flowing to the ground
Communication in harmony
In air's domain of speech and sound

Loving vows I now renew

With passion, peace, and open heart

And pledge with words of power true

That willingly I do my part

So mote it be

Something to Think About:

What do you and your partner argue about? Are the issues really important? Are you struggling for power or just falling into the habit of disagreement? What would happen if you simply chose not to argue?

Something to Try:

If you don't already do it, set aside at least fifteen minutes a day to talk to each other. Make sure each person gets equal time. If you have trouble listening to each other well, try using a speaking stick and taking turns, just as you would in circle. If you're having a really rough time, try doing this in sacred space.

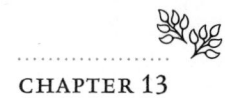

Raising Pagan Children

Parenting may be the most difficult job in the world. The hours are long, the pay is dreadful, and if you do it well, no one has any idea how hard you are working.

On the other hand, the rewards can be equally great. After all, you are raising the next generation of well-balanced, well-educated, and freethinking individuals who will go out and make invaluable contributions to the world. (And don't forget all those quiet cuddles. They are pretty wonderful too.)

But if being a parent is tough, being a Pagan parent can be even tougher. You may have to deal with a few quandaries mainstream moms and dads never even consider.

Do I tell my child about my religion, and if so, how do I explain it so that he can understand? If I am not out of the broom closet, how do I make my child understand the need for secrecy without shame or fearfulness? If she is open about "Mom or Dad the Witch" at school, will my child be ridiculed or ostracized? How much of my religion do I share with my child, and at what age should he or she be able to make a decision about whether or not to follow the Pagan path?

These are hard questions to deal with, and there is no one right or wrong answer. Parents have to make decisions based on their particular circumstances and priorities, and do their best to balance the needs of their children with how they wish to integrate their spiritual beliefs with the rest of their lives.

There are, however, a few basic suggestions and guidelines that the Pagan parent might find helpful. There are also a couple of books available that cover the topic in much more depth than we have space for here (see page 130 for some recommendations). For now, we will simply try to address the questions raised above.

Explaining Wicca/Paganism to Children

How much you tell your child (or children) about your spiritual practices will depend in part on how big a role these practices play in your day-to-day life. For instance, if you live with a non-Pagan partner and celebrate full moons and sabbats as a solitary, with little or no Pagan symbolism around the house, you may decide not to bring up the subject until your child is old enough to start asking questions about religion on his own. This is especially likely to be the case if the non-Pagan partner is uncomfortable with your being a Witch.

On the other hand, if you and your partner are both actively living a Pagan lifestyle, or you're a single parent who is out of the broom closet and practicing openly in your home, you will undoubtedly need to find some way to explain Witchcraft to the rest of the family.

With young children, it is best to keep explanations as simple as possible. Most of the Pagans I know who have toddlers don't talk much about the specifics of Witchcraft. Instead, they stress the importance of our connection with nature. God and goddess may be mentioned but not explained in detail.

Once children are old enough to start really asking questions (anywhere from around four, with the precocious ones, to seven or eight), it may be easiest to simply wait until the questions arise, and then answer them the best you can. Be honest, speak from the heart, and try to keep the concepts on a level that a child can understand.

Say, for example, that your child is included in a sabbat ritual (as all the kids belonging to Blue Moon Circle are) and asks why we call the quarters. You can answer that we want to connect with earth, air, fire, and water because they are all around us, and give a few specific examples of how the elements benefit our lives. Or you can say that we are asking them to help guard the circle and keep us safe. (If you have a big, friendly dog, you can compare it to that.)

Keep in mind that if you have included your children in rituals and celebrations from a very early age, they may not ask questions at all. After all, an integrated spiritual practice is just another facet of everyday life. Or they may, in fact, come up with answers of their own. Children can be remarkably intuitive and insightful when no one is quashing their imaginations or telling them that what they think is real is only make-believe. Pay attention to your kids—who knows, you might even learn something from them, instead of the other way around.

Of course, when children get older, you will want to talk about your religious/spiritual beliefs in more detail. Older children can understand much more of the specifics of Witchcraft, including the philosophy, history, and purpose of whichever practices you follow. The important thing to remember here is free will.

This concept applies as much to your own children as it does to other adults. (At least as far as spiritual practices are concerned. For the tattoo/piercing/makeup/dating arguments, you're on your own. That's a whole other book.)

While it is desirable to have your children understand what you believe and the importance of your practice to your life, it is not something that you should ever force on them. If young children seem afraid or overwhelmed in circle, don't make them take part. If older children and teens don't want anything to do with Witchcraft, then they should be allowed not to participate. So explain, yes, but don't push. We'll talk a bit more about this later.

Remember that the Pagan community can be a source for answers about parenting questions. After all, many others have walked this path before you, and they may have wisdom that will help you to find your way. If you are not fortunate enough to have local Pagan resources to call on, in this age of the World Wide Web, other Witches are only a mouse-click away. Just make sure that you listen to your own internal sense of right and wrong when picking which of the many voices to follow.

Secrecy Without Shame

Many of the Witches I know are openly Pagan at home. The whole family practices together, goes to ritual gatherings with friends, and integrates the love of nature into their everyday lives. However, not all of these folks are as open outside the home. Some of them are employed in areas where being out of the broom closet could jeopardize their jobs (teachers and nurses in small rural communities, for instance, are often not free to be open about their religion).

This means explaining to their children that it isn't a good idea to talk about Witchcraft, Paganism, or Mummy's coven at school. But how do you ask a child to keep your spiritual beliefs a secret without making her feel that these beliefs are somehow something to be feared or ashamed of? This has been a quandary for Pagans throughout the years, since secrecy has been an unfortunate necessity for many. In truth, we are probably living in the most open time there has ever been for Witches, but that doesn't mean that we will be accepted everywhere or by everyone.

If you decide that you are one of the folks who need to stay in the shadows for now, the first thing to consider is whether or not your children can keep a secret. Some can, even at an early age. Some can't, no matter how old they are. If secrecy is vital, you might be better off not burdening them with the necessity to keep things from their teachers and friends.

If, however, the child is included in your practice, you will have to sit down and have a talk (or talks) about the importance of not telling others. Try putting as positive a spin as possible on the situation: "This is something special that is just for us, a secret that we share together," for instance, rather than "Everyone is out to get us." A younger child may understand not talking about private matters more if you make it a game or a challenge. Older kids can be honestly and openly told about the history of Witches, the misunderstandings that still surround our practices, and the specific reasons why you feel that it is important for your beliefs to remain a secret for now.

The most crucial element of any explanation is your approach. If you teach your children that all Christians hate us and are to be feared, for example, you are not only maligning the many Christians for whom this is untrue and creating feelings of fearfulness in your child but also perpetuating the very elements of prejudice and hate that we are trying to surmount ourselves. Try to address the entire issue with as much of a positive attitude as possible. Hate and distrust only breed more of the same. Rise above them.

Living Openly at School and with Friends

Being in the broom closet can be tough, but being openly Pagan comes with its own set of challenges. Children may face ignorance and prejudice at school, or they may feel left out when there are celebrations of everyone else's holidays but not theirs.

As a parent, you try to do your best to balance being true to your own beliefs and practices with doing whatever you can to make things easier on your child. Again, there are no hard and fast rules to follow here—each parent has to make decisions based on the particular set of circumstances they face.

You may want to talk to your child about the difference between "not hiding" and "shoving things in other people's faces." After all, generally speaking, school is not an appropriate place to discuss religion. (Unless you are attending a Catholic school, which is unlikely if you are a Witch!) For the most part, kids can go through the average school day without knowing if the boy at the next desk is a Methodist or a Jew.

If religion does come up as a part of a discussion at school, you may want to prepare your child with a few simple explanations of your practices and beliefs. Let's face it: it can be difficult enough to explain Witchcraft (in whichever permutation you follow) if you are an adult; for a child, it can be even harder to put into words.

Try talking to your kids ahead of time about what being a Pagan means to them, and come up with something simple and nonthreatening for them to share with others. Emphasizing the connection to nature, for instance, is a good way to go in this increasingly "green"-aware world. And you can talk about the traditions in other cultures of worshipping both a goddess and a god; most kids study Greek mythology sooner or later, and Native American, Hindu, and Egyptian cultures also may be good examples.

You can also talk about the history of White Witches as healers and herbalists. And there's always Harry Potter, of course, although your child probably should mention that most of us can't actually make brooms fly (drat!).

What if someone picks on your children because of their religion? Well, kids get picked on for a lot of reasons, and the reaction is pretty much the same no matter what the cause: you do your best to comfort your child, help him to understand that people say mean things because they are ignorant or afraid… and then give him a cookie. (What, you thought I had some magickal answer to schoolyard bullying? Man, I wish.)

Of course, if a teacher gives your child a hard time because he or she comes from a Pagan home, that is an entirely different kettle of fish, and you are within your rights to take a grievance to the principal, the school board, or even to court. Let's hope it never comes to that, and that any problems that do arise can be solved by calm, reasonable conversation.

Holidays at school can be tough for the kids who don't follow the popular religions. I grew up Jewish in an area that had very few Jews, in the days before it became politically correct to have "equal opportunity" celebrations. It was pretty much Christmas for everyone, regardless. No one understood why I didn't know the words to the carols (or care to sing them, for that matter), and the teachers never considered that there might be a child who didn't want to write to Santa or make a Christmas stocking to hang up.

Things are a little easier these days, although most teachers will probably still not think to include the less mainstream religions. If your child's teacher is reasonably open-minded, you may want to talk to him or her about including Yule in the Christmas/Chanukkah/Kwanza lineup come December. And at home, you may celebrate both the Pagan holidays and the important days from the religion you were raised in or that a partner still follows.

Keep in mind that many of the holidays that are widely celebrated have Pagan roots; it may help to explain to your child that the Easter Bunny is carrying Ostara eggs!

Sharing the Pagan World with Children

As parents, we want to share the things we love and value with our children. For some that might mean an appreciation for outdoor sports, for others a love of reading, music, or art. As Witches, most of us also want to share this wonderful spiritual path we've found.

And rightly so. But just as there are some of life's treasures that we wouldn't introduce our children to just yet—like single-malt scotch or driving fast cars—there are some aspects of Wicca/Paganism that might not be suitable for the younger set.

Depending on your own particular practice, Witchcraft can have a darker aspect that might scare small children. It might be better to wait until they are older and can better understand some of the more complicated issues before showing them a picture of Hecate wearing her necklace of testicles, for example. (Especially if your child is a boy. Can you say "therapy"?)

In general, however, it is fairly easy to decide whether or not to include your child in a ritual performed in your own home. After all, in this case, you are in control of both the magickal working and the kid in question, at least theoretically. And any rituals performed by a group will usually be intended to be child-friendly or not, depending on the occasion, and you should be able to find out ahead of time from the high priest or high priestess. (Assuming you are not running them yourself.)

Blue Moon Circle has a general rule of thumb: sabbat rituals are intended for the whole family (including a variety of small children and only semi-Pagan husbands) and are written accordingly. Full moons and new moons, on the other hand, tend to be used for more serious magickal work, and we usually ask people not to bring their kids (with the exception of babies who are breastfed, who usually come to circle until they are toddling around and grabbing at candles).

This is a clear rule, and therefore we've never had a problem with it. If you practice with a group, communication about this issue is important; not everyone wants to mix magick with minors (especially if they don't have children of their own).

Those of us in Blue Moon Circle all agree that you can't raise Pagan children without including them in some ritual activities, especially those that celebrate the holidays. But every group is different, so before bringing your child to a ritual put on by folks you don't know all that well, it is best to check ahead of time and make sure children are welcome and no unsuitable activities are planned.

This brings us to the large public gatherings. There are many of these, some of which can be huge. And while it may be tempting to share the special occasion of a coming together of the clans with your children, there are a few things you should probably consider first.

To begin with, how well does your child react to that many people? Will he or she be thrilled or overwhelmed? If there is nudity, will that be a problem? Is this the kind of gathering at which there is likely to be overt sexual energy or drug use? Will your child be confused by the many varieties of theology, some of which may not bear much resemblance to whatever you practice at home?

I'm not saying that you shouldn't take a child to these celebrations. I'm just suggesting that you look into the details of any particular gathering before you go, and make a decision based both on the information you garner and your own personal knowledge of your child. Large crowds of Witches can generate an amazing amount of energy—something even adults can have a hard time handling. You might want to plan ahead so that you retreat to your own campsite at night when things get rowdy. (What, Witches rowdy? Not us. Well, hardly ever.)

As far as your practices at home are concerned, it is up to you to decide how much of your spiritual practice it is wise to share with your children. Certainly it is safe for anyone and everyone to pass on the love of nature and an appreciation for Mother Earth. Beyond that, most of the basic Pagan beliefs and practices are fairly benign, and those that might be harmful to children are easily left for more private moments.

There are some situations, however, in which the choice will not be entirely up to you, alas. I know a Witch whose custody battle got pretty nasty when it came to the issue of him bringing his daughter to rituals. The girl had been brought up Wiccan and had gone to rituals since she was a baby, but the estranged mom was a Christian and insisted that the child never be included in any Pagan activities. Unfortunately, the judge agreed with her and left the Witch dad with no other options. If he tried to follow his heart instead of the law, he ran the risk of losing any visitation with his child.

In cases like this, there is little a Pagan parent can do. But that doesn't mean that you can't share the basic values of your spiritual beliefs. You may not be able to explain them in terms that are associated with Witchcraft, but no one can stop you from teaching your child not to harm others, to be responsible for their own actions, to put out into the universe what they want to get back, and to love nature. These ideas are universal and positive, and can be shared with children no matter what the circumstances.

When Your Child Decides to Be a Witch

Your child may have attended rituals from the time that she was a baby, but that doesn't make her a Witch. (Just cute as the dickens in her little pointy hat.)

Being a Witch is a choice, one that no one can make for another human being. There are differing opinions about when a child is old enough to make this choice; some people think at thirteen (much like a Jewish child has a bar/ bat mitzvah at this age to mark leaving childhood behind and becoming an adult), while others believe that eighteen is the magick number.

I'm not sure it is as simple as one number or another. Yes, our society says that a child becomes a legal adult at eighteen. At eighteen you can vote, serve in the armed forces, and, in many states, get married. My guess is that by then you can also decide whether or not you are a Witch.

But some children grow up faster and are capable of making even crucial decisions like this one at seventeen or even sixteen. And there are some folks who never grow up and bounce from religion to religion as if each commitment was like a temporary ticket to get on a ride at the amusement park.

So how do you know if your child is ready? And if you are a teen, how do you know that you are ready to make this choice?

I believe that this is a matter of both common sense and of faith. If a child tends to be rock-steady in most of his decisions, follows through on his commitments, and understands the serious nature of the vow he intends to make, then he is probably ready. On the other hand, if he is a child who swings from one choice to another, is undependable in everyday activities, and rarely honors a promise, then undoubtedly he is not.

This is the commonsense part. The faith part is a little trickier. Many children are a bit of both types mentioned above. So how do you know if they are serious about this particular choice?

Pretty much the same way you know that an adult who chooses to be a Witch is serious, really. Have they been practicing for at least a year and a day? Have they learned the basic tenets of their particular path and started more in-depth study? Do they take their spiritual practice seriously, devoting time and energy to it?

If the answer to all these questions is yes, and you ask the gods for their guidance and they agree, then the child is probably ready, whether he or she is eighteen or not.

Of course, this may only apply if you are talking about your own child. If you are a high priest or high priestess and a child not your own comes to you and asks to be initiated, things get a bit trickier. I know group leaders who will not allow children under eighteen to attend circle without the permission of their parents, because they are worried about getting into legal hot water. This is a legitimate fear and one not to be taken lightly.

On the other hand, I know other groups that routinely include teens who are underage and don't seem to have a problem. There are many teens these days who are interested in Wicca and Paganism, and the leaders of these groups feel that teens should have the right to learn and practice, just like anyone else. This is a tough decision, and one I am thankful that I have never had to make. Again, this is something that you might consider bringing to the gods, and then accept whatever answer they give you as the best way to proceed.

Not all children take to Witchcraft right away. They may experiment with other religious choices, or practice nothing at all, then eventually come back and decide to be Witches. And if you came to Witchcraft later in life, as I did, you may not have raised your child as a Pagan. What then? Do you pressure or encourage your children to join you on your new path? Do you leave them to find their own way with no help at all?

Well, here's what happened in my case, just as an example.

By the time I realized I was a Witch, I was already in my thirties. My step-daughter (her dad and I divorced when she was five, but we kept a close relationship both then and now) was in her teens and following her own path. I was honest with her about my beliefs and shared some of my experiences with her but never particularly tried to include her in any Pagan activities, in part because her father is a serious born-again Christian these days.

A few years ago, when she was in her early twenties, she started expressing mild interest in Wicca. She'd been studying Buddhism for a number of years (a path I'd followed previously as well) and was curious to see what the two spiritual paths had in common. So I lent her a couple of basic books, and we had a few discussions about the subject. And then I left her alone.

This was the tough part. I really wanted to share this amazing part of my life with her. I believed that it would help her tackle some of the issues she was struggling with and that she was incredibly suited to be a Witch. But she loves and respects me, and considers me to be a role model in many ways.

Not that this is a bad thing—quite the contrary. But my concern was that if I encouraged her too much, she'd decide to become a Witch to please me and not to please herself. And I believe strongly that each of us has to come to Witchcraft on our own, in our own time. I also believe that if we are meant to walk this path, the gods will guide us to it.

So I waited, and I hoped, but I did nothing.

And in time, she came to me and asked to attend a ritual. Then another. These days, she is a regular participant in circle, practices magick on her own, and even traveled across the country with me to attend PantheaCon, a major Pagan convention in San Jose. She told me just the other day that she believed that being a Witch was helping her to become a better person and to find her way in the world.

A mother couldn't ask for more than that. In the end, we want our children to be happy and healthy. And whether or not that means they walk the Pagan path is up to them and to the gods themselves.

Something to Try:

If you are raising children in a Pagan tradition, you may want to read one of the following books:

Raising Witches: Teaching the Wiccan Faith to Children by Ashleen O'Gaea

The Family Wicca Book: The Craft for Parents & Children by Ashleen O'Gaea

Circle Round: Raising Children in Goddess Traditions by Starhawk, Diane Baker, and Anne Hill

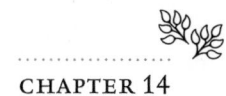

Interacting with Others
at Work and at Play

Issues of Prejudice and Tolerance

Merriam-Webster's Dictionary defines prejudice as "preconceived judgment or opinion, an adverse opinion or leaning formed without grounds or before sufficient knowledge, an irrational attitude or hostility directed against an individual, a group, a race or their supposed characteristics."

Irrational is pretty much the keyword here. Prejudice doesn't have anything to do with rational thought. It is based in ignorance, fear, and hate—all bad stuff, as far as I am concerned, and definitely irrational.

If you are living openly as a Witch, sooner or later you are going to run into prejudice—probably sooner. How much and how bad it is will depend in part on factors like where you live and who you generally associate with, as well as how "out" you actually are as a Pagan. A discreet pentacle around your neck will draw a lot less attention than a giant horned god tattoo on your arm and a bumper sticker that reads, "Doing my bit to piss off the religious right." (I love that one. But no, it's not on my car.)

To some extent, you can control how much prejudice you will face; you can keep a lower profile if you live in an area that is predominately Christian and conservative, for instance, or be openly Pagan in your social life but not at work.

I am pretty fortunate in my own situation. Although I live in a generally conservative area (more Republicans than Democrats, and over twenty churches of one denomination or another in my little town alone), there are two colleges here as well, which tend to draw a more liberal element.

My "day job" is as executive director and manager of the Artisans' Guild, a local cooperative shop that a friend and I founded almost ten years ago. In addition to running the shop, I also make jewelry as one of the fifty artists/members—and people expect artists to be a little odd and unconventional, so no one is all that worried about my being a Witch.

I am firmly out of the broom closet; my previous books are on display right next to my jewelry, and I usually wear one of the pentacle necklaces I design. Most of the customers and the other artists seem to take it all in stride.

On the other hand, I make an effort to be low-key about the whole thing and never impose my personal beliefs on the store as a whole. Although we have a number of Pagan members, most of the artists follow more conventional religious paths, and it wouldn't be fair to turn the shop in a direction that would make many of its members uncomfortable.

I do get a number of questions from the curious, and every once in a while someone looks at me a little strangely, but for the most part, my being a Witch hasn't caused a problem. Even my born-again Christian ex-in-laws seem to accept me as I am.

Not everyone is this lucky, however, and most Witches run into prejudice from time to time. (It happens to me too, but thankfully just not often.) I believe most prejudice stems from one of two sources: ignorance and hatred. These two things are not mutually exclusive, of course, and some people manage both at once, but one or the other is usually dominant.

Of the two, ignorance is probably easier to deal with and more likely to be fixable. Someone who believes the traditional propaganda about Witches worshipping the devil can be educated about the differences between Witches and Satanists, informed that Witches don't even believe in Satan, and told about the rule of "harm none." If the person in question has a reasonably open mind, it is possible to turn prejudice into tolerance, and eventually, maybe even to acceptance.

The best way to respond to prejudice that stems from ignorance is to be polite, friendly, and nonconfrontational. Remember that every opportunity you take to re-educate and enlighten someone who doesn't understand us benefits the Pagan community as a whole. And while we do not believe in pushing our religion on anyone else, we do believe in spreading the light of truth about Wicca, Paganism, and Witchcraft.

Prejudice that is rooted in hatred can be more difficult to deal with. Hatred comes from fear, and fear is much more difficult to eliminate than ignorance. (Think about the prejudice that has been aimed at Jews, African Americans, and various other ethnic and religious groups over the centuries.)

Fear is irrational and often has roots that run deep into childhood and the way we were brought up. It is one thing to watch a lot of bad Hollywood movies about so-called Satanic Witches and another thing entirely to be raised to believe that anyone who calls themselves a Witch is evil and untrustworthy.

You might be able to talk sense to the person who watched too many bad movies; most people realize that much of what they see on the big screen is imaginary. But how do you change the mind of someone who is absolutely certain that you are a threat to everything that they believe in?

Sadly, sometimes you can't. If you are fortunate, you may be able to arrive at some sort of truce and agree to disagree.

As I mentioned before, my ex-in-laws are born-again Christians, as is my ex-brother-in-law, whom I consider a friend. We get along fine as long as we avoid a few tricky topics of conversation, like most issues of politics and religion. I know that he thinks I have a weird religion. He knows that I think he has a weird religion. We also have a genuine affection for each other and have simply decided not to let our differences stand in the way of our friendship.

But what if you come up against prejudice that you can't learn to live with or someone who refuses to accept that it is possible to be both a Witch and a decent human being?

Well, obviously, if the situation is temporary or unimportant, like someone you happen to end up talking to at a party, the best thing to do is shrug and walk away. After all, you can't please everyone all the time. And if you can't change the person's mind, there is not much to be gained by banging your head against a brick wall. (Unless you happen to like that kind of thing.)

If you are in a situation you can't walk away from, like having a coworker who dislikes or distrusts you simply because you are a Witch—and not just because you keep taking the last doughnut—that can be a great deal tougher.

In such a case, the best that you can hope for is that by consistently behaving in a pleasant, professional, and honorable manner, you will prove to your coworker that his fears and biases are unfounded. Of course, you could be unpleasant, argumentative, and occasionally threaten to turn him into a toad, but that is hardly likely to improve things, now, is it?

There are going to be times when prejudice is a serious problem, but I can't think of any instance when responding with calmness and courtesy isn't the best way to cope.

Let's face it; there are plenty of people out there who have no idea—or all the wrong ideas—of what it means to be a Witch. The best way that we can combat prejudice is to show the world that we are human beings just like them; that we love our partners and our children, harm none, value our word, and try to live our beliefs in a positive and life-affirming way.

If prejudice is based on ignorance and fear, our best bet at getting rid of it is to educate those around us and show them that there is nothing to be afraid of. There is, however, one response to prejudice that never, ever works, and that is to hate back.

There was an incidence of prejudice I came across this week that particularly resonated with this topic. I thought it was an interesting "coincidence" that it happened to come up just as I was writing this chapter—obviously, the gods thought I was missing the bigger picture.

You see, the prejudice in this case wasn't coming from one of "them." It came from one of "us."

I was at my local credit union, chatting with one of the women who worked there as she processed my deposit. She noticed my pentacle and mentioned that she, too, was a Witch, although she didn't practice as much now as she used to. In the course of our conversation, we talked about a few different Pagan topics, and she seemed quite pleasant. Right up until the point when she said vehemently, "I hate Catholics."

Ouch. Since I didn't know this woman, and we were in a public, professional setting, I didn't feel free to get into a major discussion on the matter, so I just ignored it, finished my business, and left. But what I really wanted to say was this: "You've met every Catholic there is? Really? Because otherwise, how could you be sure you hate them all? And isn't *hate* a pretty rough word?"

Clearly, this woman felt strongly about Catholics. I'm guessing that at some point she'd had a bad experience, or maybe more than one, with someone who was Catholic. But to decide that all Catholics were terrible and worthy of such a negative emotion as hate (and to feel so strongly about it that she would tell a complete stranger) was almost certainly not merited by whatever that experience had been.

She's not the first Pagan I've come across who harbored strong negative feelings and opinions toward other established religions or Christians in particular. There are plenty of Witches who are still mad at all Christians because of the Burning Times, for instance. But that would be as if I hated all Germans because of the Holocaust, which would be just ridiculous. Heck, most of the Germans alive now weren't even born when that happened, and you know none of the current Christians were around for the Burning Times.

Yes, there are some folks who are prejudiced against Witches, and certainly the more fundamental Christians often feed the fires of ignorance and hatred. But do we really want to stand around those fires and add our own fear, anger, and close-mindedness to the flames? I sure as Hades hope not.

Instead, let's act toward others as we would like them to act toward us. (Yes, that's the familiar Golden Rule—Do unto others as you would have them do unto you.) Remember that all of us are human beings, flawed and imperfect. And yet we have much more in common with each other than we have things that set us apart. And the gods love us all, no matter what religious path we happen to choose, and I firmly believe they want us to love each other.

So let us walk away from the fire of prejudice, which will only turn around and burn us in the end. Instead, let's send out the warmth of love and kindness. Remember, what you put out is what comes back to you. Which would you rather have when it comes around again? I vote love. How about you?

Something to Think About:

Is there any group of people that you are prejudiced against? Did that group as a whole do something to harm you, or was it really just one or two people? Did they act out of ignorance or fear? If it was ignorance, is there anything that you can do to educate them? If it was fear, can you make them less afraid? And if you can't, can you turn your hatred into compassion? After all, think how unpleasant it is to be afraid.

Something to Try:

If you know someone who is prejudiced against you because you are a Witch, try reaching out to them. Maybe you can find some common ground, like a love of gardening, pets, or your children. If the situation is so bad that you do not feel you can reach out in person, try taking a few moments every day to visualize them and send them love. (Keep in mind that you do not need to like someone in order to love them.) You might be surprised at what happens. This simple act can sometimes work miracles.

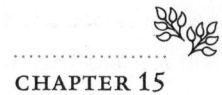

Out of the Broom Closet
Whom to Tell and When

If coming out of the broom closet means exposing yourself to prejudice, mis-understanding, and maybe worse, why on earth would anyone do it? Why not leave our pentacles at home and go about our business in the outside world with no one the wiser? After all, we can always practice our religion quietly, in the privacy of our own homes, where no one can see us.

It's a good question, really. And for some people, the right answer is to stay in the closet. In many cases, that has more to do with circumstances than with an individual Witch's preference, but there are plenty of folks who just see their religion as a private, personal thing and nobody else's business.

And they are right. If you decide that you don't want anyone else to know about your Pagan beliefs and practices, or if you wish to share this part of your life only with close friends and family, that is a legitimate choice. Don't let any-one tell you otherwise.

There is nothing in the Craft that requires its practitioners to be out of the broom closet—in fact, we mostly have a history of staying hidden. Which, to my mind, is the best reason to stop doing so. All that prejudice, ignorance and hatred exists, in part, because we stayed hidden for so long. Not only are things that lurk in the shadows scary, but you can't dispel people's misconceptions about you if they can't see you.

I always smile when someone says to me, "You're the first Witch I've ever met," because I'm fairly certain I'm not. People come into contact with Witches every day: nurses, teachers, store clerks, waitresses, plumbers, and mechanics. Most of these folks are probably liked and accepted. But since no one knows that the nice guy next door or the friendly woman at work is also a Pagan, Witches are still getting a bad rap.

The only way we will ever be accepted by the rest of society is if we step out of the shadows and show ourselves as the wonderful, loving, productive Everyday Witches that we are.

So how do you know if it is the right time for you to come out of the broom closet, and what is the best way to do so once you've made up your mind?

Well, let's start with a few things *not* to do:

- Tell your fiancé and his entire family that you are a Witch at the rehearsal dinner the night before your wedding.
- Inform your potential boss you are a Pagan during a job interview.
- Announce to your soon-to-be-ex-congregation at Sunday services that you are leaving to join a coven.
- Stand up in the midst of the PTA meeting to protest the school Christmas pageant.

What's wrong with all these scenarios? We'll take them one by one.

Tell your fiancé and his entire family that you are a Witch at the rehearsal dinner the night before your wedding...

There are two problems with this situation. The first is that, if you are about to be married, you should have shared this information with your partner long before you embarked on a life together. Being a Witch is an important part of who you are and should never be kept a secret from someone with whom you are seriously involved. If he (or she) can't handle the truth about you, then he's not the right one for you. After all, would you want to be married to someone and find out one day that he never told you he was, say, a Russian spy? Or a Republican?

Rule #1: It's not okay to stay in the broom closet with someone you love once you are seriously involved. You don't have to mention it on your first date, but you'll have to sooner or later, and a close relationship requires honesty about who and what you truly are. And once you realize things are getting serious, sooner is probably better than later. (Hey, if Mr. Wonderful is going to run for the hills at the first glimpse of a pointy hat, wouldn't you rather know it before you spend months picking out furniture together?)

Now, about the in-laws. This is a little trickier. In some cases, it might be better to allow the new family to get to know you before letting them in on your Pagan secret identity. On the other hand, if they already like and accept you, they will probably take the news of your unconventional religious practices in stride. As long as you don't hit them with it at a bad moment, like the night before the wedding.

Rule #2: Timing is everything. As with most important decisions in life, you want to give careful thought to the where and when of coming out of the broom closet. Most of the time, it is better to talk to people individually rather than in groups, and not to spring it on them during situations that are already filled with tension.

For instance, don't stand at Aunt Tillie's graveside and pronounce to everyone that she's in the Summerland and will come back again in her next incarnation. If there is someone in the family whom you think will be comforted by that information, talk to them later, when the two of you can discuss the concept more fully. Here's a good rule of thumb: if you're not sure if this situation is appropriate, it probably isn't.

Inform your potential boss that you are a Pagan during a job interview…

This one also falls under the "situation not appropriate" category. Unless you are applying for a job as a tarot reader, or something along those lines, your being a Pagan has no bearing on the kind of job you would do. You wouldn't expect someone applying for a secretary's position to say, "I can type 100 words a minute, and I'm a Protestant," after all.

And, sadly, you might not get the job. Again, it is better to let the boss get to know you before letting the black cat out of the bag. This doesn't mean that if you always wear a pentacle, you have to take it off for the interview—that's up to you. But in certain situations, it is best not to make an issue of your religion, no matter what it happens to be.

Rule #3: In some situations, mentioning religion is just not appropriate. Religion is, in essence, a private matter. And just as there are situations when it is not appropriate to share other personal issues (such as your sexual preferences or having a handicap, or anything else that isn't relative to the situation at hand), there are times when it is better not to come out of the broom closet. If you are applying for a job, a loan, or to rent an apartment, for instance, it is no one's business what your spiritual practices are—regardless of whether bringing them up could get you rejected. Just because people are not legally allowed to discriminate on the grounds of religion doesn't mean it doesn't happen every day. Pick your battles carefully.

Announce to your soon-to-be-ex-congregation at Sunday services that you are leaving to join a coven…

If you've decided that the religious path you are on is no longer the right one for you, that's fine. People are entitled to change their minds. You don't owe anyone an explanation, although people might ask you for one. But in cases like this, try not to be confrontational. If you are leaving, just leave.

Rule #4: Use a little tact. Say, for instance, that you've decided it is time to tell your parents that you are a Witch. Whether you are sixteen or forty-six, this can be a difficult conversation. If you start out by saying, "Going to church is torture, I don't believe any of the things you believe, and I am going to be a Witch instead," your folks will undoubtedly be upset and defensive.

On the other hand, if you say, "I respect your beliefs, but after much soul-searching, I've decided I prefer another path," you've at least left some room for calm discussion.

Keep in mind that both of these statements may be equally true—but one is considerably more tactful than the other and far more likely to get you positive results.

Coming out of the broom closet doesn't have to be unpleasant. In many cases, people will greet your announcement with openness and acceptance. When I told my parents, they weren't upset in the least. They thought I was a little weird, maybe, but hey, they've always thought that. (And they may have a point.)

What's important is that you approach whomever you're telling in a calm, rational, and nonconfrontational manner. Be positive ("I have never felt this good about myself before") rather than negative ("I hate your view of a stern, patriarchal god"). Talk about why being a Pagan works for you; explain your fundamental beliefs—with an emphasis on "harm none" if necessary—and explain that having these beliefs doesn't change who you are or how you feel about them.

Be loving and patient, and try not to get into an argument. The person you are telling will either accept the news with good grace or not; getting into a fight over it will only make things worse, as well as make it more difficult for them to be more accepting later on.

Which brings us to Rule #5: There are some people who are never going to be happy about you being out of the broom closet. You can certainly go ahead and tell them anyway, but be prepared for the consequences. I've known people who've lost long-time friendships because a staunchly Christian friend couldn't come to terms with their involvement in the Craft.

While there are many people who will accept you as you are, there will always be a few who won't be able to deal with it. Only you can decide whether or not it is worth the risk to tell someone you know for certain will disapprove strongly. You have the right to be honest about who you are—but others have the right to walk away once they know you are a Witch, if that fact is something they can't live with. And some people might surprise you.

Stand up in the midst of the PTA meeting to protest the school Christmas pageant…

Yes, you have the right to your religious beliefs. And you have the right to live those beliefs in whichever way you see fit. But so does everyone else. Try to get your religion included without attacking those religions that already are.

Rule # 6: Standing up for your religion doesn't entitle you to insult somebody else's. Paganism is not the predominant religious path in this country, and it probably never will be (despite Wicca being the fastest-growing religion in the United States and Canada). And while political correctness has expanded the realm of "acceptable" religions to include a whole group of folks who never used to be in the mainstream, it may be some time before Wicca and Neopaganism are added to that list.

So it might be tempting, while you're sitting there listening to them plan the Christmas pageant and adding in a Hanukkah song and a Kwanzaa candle-lighting ceremony so they don't offend anyone, to jump up in protest of the unfairness of it all. You might want to tell them that your child's religion is being excluded, and unless she is allowed to take part, you will sue the school system for discrimination.

Probably not helpful, all things considered.

After all, those folks have the right to celebrate their religions too. And yes, it would be nice if they would include us in the celebrations, but in many locales that simply isn't something a school system could get away with—at least not without a huge uproar and upsetting a lot of other folks. Someday, maybe, but not today.

If you want to try to persuade the school to include a Pagan element, you might try talking to the teacher in charge of the pageant and asking if it would be possible to insert a skit about the battle between the Oak King and the Holly King, or a light theatrical explanation of how many of the origins of Christmas were derived from the Pagan holiday of Yule.

You could talk to the principal about the fact that Wicca is a legally recognized religion, and point out that there are a growing number of Pagan families in your school system. But remember that old saying "You catch more flies with honey," and try complimenting them on their open-mindedness for including many religions, rather than berating them for overlooking yours.

No matter what the situation is, don't forget the law of returns; acceptance begets acceptance. Being out of the broom closet means being open about your religion—it shouldn't mean being critical of anyone else's.

There is no perfect time or place to come out of the broom closet, and only you can decide if such an action is appropriate for you in your own particular circumstances. When in doubt, ask the gods for guidance, and listen closely to your own inner wisdom.

And keep in mind that once you are out of the broom closet, you represent the Pagan community as a whole, standing in for its many members who must still remain in the shadows for now.

Something to Try:

If you are considering coming out of the broom closet, start with the people who you can be fairly certain will accept the news easily. Once you have had a few successful conversations on the subject, it will be easier to tackle the more difficult ones. If you are having a hard time coming up with the right words, you may want to try writing it down first, or even practice in front of a mirror or with another Pagan friend.

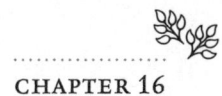

Representing Pagans in the Outside World

Here is a hard truth: if you are a member of a minority, every impression counts; you need to put your best foot forward.

Pagans face an interesting challenge as they interact with mainstream society. On the one hand, we are mostly a bunch of semi-quirky individualists, often set apart from most other folks by our independence, unusual beliefs, and—in many cases—downright weirdness. (Let's hear it for weirdness! Huzzah, huzzah!)

On the other hand, since there are so few of us who are currently living openly as Pagans, and since Witches and Pagans tend to have a bad reputation with the mundanes in general, it is important that all of us who are "out of the broom closet" serve as the best possible example for the Pagan community we represent.

How on earth are we to reconcile these two aspects of Pagan existence? Is it possible to be true to our nontraditional, think-outside-the-box selves and still find a way to make a good impression on the rest of society?

Yes, I think it is possible. And what's more, I believe that it is absolutely necessary. If we are ever going to be accepted by others as equals to be respected, rather than oddballs to be feared or ridiculed, we have to show those around us that Witches are worthy of that respect.

What does this mean to the Everyday Witch?

It means that we need to follow the few rules we have set for ourselves: that we harm none, are true to our word, live in harmony with nature and our fellow human beings, respect the gods and each other, and generally walk our talk.

If we want others to take us seriously, we have to take ourselves seriously. Sometimes that means choosing when to be weird (huzzah!) and when not to stand out from the crowd.

It means remaining aware that each time we say out loud to a stranger, "I am a Witch," that there are hundreds of other Witches standing in the shadows who will be judged by the actions that follow that statement.

I am not going to tell anyone how to live their life or how to behave. That is a matter between you, your conscience, and your gods.

But I will urge every Pagan who is living openly to consider the effect that your words and deeds will have on the rest of the Pagan community.

You are our voice, our emissary, and our link to the outside world. You can forge the bonds that will enable the many who walk the path after you to enter the mundane world with heads held high and hearts wide open.

You have the opportunity to dispel fear and prejudice, replace ignorance with knowledge, and set an example that young Pagans will want to follow.

Be your best self.

It is true what they say: actions speak louder than words. So be true to yourself, but also be true to the beliefs that we all embrace, and go out there and make us all proud.

Something to Try:

Try to find a way in which you can contribute something to your community and set an example of how a Pagan can be a positive force for good. Many Pagan groups collect canned goods for local food banks when they hold public gatherings, for instance. Pagan groups can also raise money for local charities or adopt a section of road or an area in a local park and keep it clean. If you are a Solitary, you can volunteer in a home for the elderly or at a local animal shelter; after all, as Pagans, we value our elders and love our animal companions. There are plenty of ways to manifest your beliefs in a concrete fashion while also proving to the world that we are "good Witches, not bad Witches."

part five

the
practicing
WITCH

God/dess in Everyone
The Essence of Being a Witch

Most Witches grew up with some variation of the standard Judeo-Christian religious beliefs. These usually featured a god who was a stern father figure, frequently unimaginable and distant—a deity one could pray to, but who might only answer back through the aid of another (almost always male) authority figure. Both in Scripture and in life, women were often looked at as being somehow lesser than men—less pure, less holy, less capable of speaking to God.

Little wonder so many of us left.

However, in Wicca and Paganism in general, the story is quite different. Well, stories, really—since there are so many different forms and versions of Pagan faith. But for the most part, Witches believe in both a goddess and a god, reflecting the balance found in the rest of the natural world.

For some, these deities are separate parts of a greater whole, while for others they are concrete symbols of a more abstract idea. But no matter how we view the god and the goddess, one thing is universally true for all the Pagans I have ever met: we need no one to help us speak to the gods or to help us hear them speak to us.

We are all priests and priestesses, capable of communion with deity on the deepest, most intimate level. What's more, just as the god and goddess are equal in power and glory, so men and women are equal, with neither subservient to the other.

Witches believe that all of us have an element of deity within us; we are each in some way god and goddess, human beings containing a spark of the divine.

This belief colors the way we practice our Craft, worship our gods, and view the universe. We are connected to the gods, and through them we are connected to each other and to the rest of the world.

There is God/dess in every one of us, and so we have both the power and the responsibility to create positive change in the world and in ourselves.

How we go about doing that is what the practice of Witchcraft is all about.

Something to Think About:

How is your practice as a Pagan different from the religious model you grew up with? Does it make you feel stronger? Can you sense that spark of deity inside?

Something to Try:

During the next full moon, stand outside under the stars and take a moment to feel the light of the goddess reflecting the deity in you. Whether you are a man or a woman, all of us have a little piece of the goddess inside. Open your heart, and feel that piece reaching out to the rest of the universe. Can you feel the universe reaching back?

The Solitary Witch

The image of the Solitary Witch stirring a cauldron under a glowing moon with a black cat her only companion is etched into our collective consciousness. And for many Witches, this is still the essential reality of their practice.

Witches who practice alone are commonly referred to as Solitaries. Some are Solitary by choice, preferring to worship and work magick on their own. Others are Solitary by default, either because they live in an area with few other Pagans or because they have not yet found a group of Witches that suits their needs and personalities.

An Eclectic Witch, for instance, would probably not feel comfortable in a coven that follows the traditional Gardnerian hierarchical degree system and vice versa, although a Green Witch and an Eclectic Witch could usually practice together quite easily.

The two women who founded Blue Moon Circle with me had both been Solitaries for over ten years, at least in part because they had never found other Witches they felt comfortable working with. And as far as I can tell, they had both been perfectly satisfied with their Solitary practice for all that time and only became "group Witches" when a group that was perfect for them finally came along.

Many Solitaries, in fact, feel absolutely no desire to practice in concert with others, except perhaps for the occasional sabbat celebration.

The Solitary Witch has a long and honorable tradition, and for many, it is the only way they desire to follow the Craft. And even those Witches who are primarily "group Witches" almost always do some kind of magickal work on their own from time to time. In this way, I suppose, all Witches can be considered Solitaries.

So what does a Solitary do? Anything he or she wants to, for the most part. Some Solitary Witches perform elaborate rituals, much as if they were in a traditional circle. Others do little more than stand out under the full moon and speak from the heart. There is no wrong answer here, and since there is no one else involved, the Solitary Witch can do as she or he pleases.

I am not going to reinvent the wheel here; there are many, many (many) books that are devoted to instructing the Solitary Witch, and I am not going to waste your time by going over material you can find in a hundred other places. So we will talk briefly about a few of the pros and cons of being a Solitary and a little bit about the Solitary path, and leave it at that.

For the most part, whether an aspect of practicing alone is a pro or a con often depends on the individual Witch. For instance, some Witches find it easier to raise energy in a group setting than they do on their own. On the other hand, there are folks who find others distracting and actually focus better on their own. It really comes down to personal preferences.

But here are a few ways in which a solitary practice of magick—even if you are usually a group Witch—can have an advantage over working with a group:

FOCUS ON YOUR OWN GOALS—If you are working by yourself, you don't have to give any thought or attention to the goals or needs of others (magickally speaking, that is) and can focus exclusively on your own personal needs at that moment.

SIMPLICITY—When working with a group, it is almost always necessary to use a formal circle if for no other reason than to contain all the energy raised. It is also helpful to get everyone focused in the same direction, something that isn't a concern when working on your own. Many Solitary Witches don't bother with complicated circle castings and simply visualize the space in which they are working as being safe and blessed.

NO PERSONALITY CONFLICTS—Let's face it: working with other people can be complicated and tricky. Even the most cooperative and easy-going of groups may run into problems with misunderstandings or people who simply don't get along.

CONVENIENCE—If you are a Solitary, you can do magickal work whenever and wherever it is needed or convenient. (As long as you can get your partner, your kids, and your in-laws out of the way, that is.) If you are in a group, there is all that scheduling to deal with—figuring out who can meet when and agreeing on what everyone wants to work on can be tricky, at best.

COMMUNION WITH THE GODS—I'm not saying that you can't make a connection with the gods from within a circle of other Witches. I do it all the time. But for some Witches, it is easier to feel that connection with deity when there is no one else around.

So if these are the advantages to being a Solitary, what are the disadvantages? Truthfully, if you are by nature a Solitary Witch, there probably aren't many. But if you are someone who would like to practice with others but simply have not yet found the right folks to work with, there are probably a few benefits you are missing out on:

FELLOWSHIP—There is nothing like looking around the circle at the firelight shining on the faces of a group of your fellow Witches and seeing your own joy reflected back at you.

ENERGY—It can be tremendously energizing to practice with others, especially in groups that work well together. No one Witch can possibly raise the same amount of energy on his or her own that a big bunch of Pagans can when working in unison.

ACCEPTANCE—It is a wonderful feeling to be surrounded by others who believe as you do. For Pagans, this can be an especially rare treat, only available to us at some form of group ritual or festival gathering.

TAKING TURNS BEING RESPONSIBLE FOR THE MAGICKAL WORKING—If you practice on your own, you are always the one who has to come up with the ritual, spell, or focus for the night's activities. When you work with a group, there will often be someone else to take on this responsibility.

These are just a few of the basic pros and cons, but what I said before is really true: it depends, for the most part, on the individual Witch and what he or she is comfortable with. I know plenty of Solitary Witches who wouldn't trade their path for one shared with others, no matter how many advantages there might be.

The truth is, if you are a Solitary at heart, nothing anyone could say will change that. Nor should it. There is no right or wrong way to worship the gods, only the way that works best for you.

Something to Try:

Here are a few books that I think can be especially helpful for the Solitary Witch:

Wicca: A Guide for the Solitary Practitioner by Scott Cunningham

Be Blessed: Daily Devotions for Busy Wiccans and Pagans by Denise Dumars

Embracing the Moon: A Witch's Guide to Ritual, Spellcraft and Shadow Work by Yasmine Galenorn

A Witch Alone: Thirteen Moons to Master Natural Magic by Marian Green

The Wicca Handbook by Eileen Holland

The Circle Within: Creating a Wiccan Spiritual Tradition by Dianne Sylvan

Your Book of Shadows: How to Write Your Own Magickal Spells by Patricia Telesco

The Group Witch

Circle, Coven, or Grove?

When people think of Witches, they often visualize a bunch of women dressed in long black cloaks, dancing around a bonfire and cackling madly. Personally, I'm not much of a cackler, but the rest of that image could certainly describe some aspects of my life as a Witch.

I am a member of a group of Witches. We most often refer to ourselves as a circle, but we occasionally use the term coven as well. The number in the group fluctuates from year to year, but we rarely have more than seven or eight of us, and the core of the group has been practicing together for over five years.

More by accident than by design, Blue Moon Circle consists (at the time of this writing, anyway) of all women, varying in age from twenty to fifty-mumble-mumble. We usually meet twice a month on new moons, full moons, and/or sabbats.

The women of Blue Moon Circle come from different backgrounds, work in different fields, and have wildly varying home lives. We don't even all look at the gods in exactly the same way.

And yet, we are as close-knit a group as I have ever seen; we accept and value each other as individuals and lend support to each other when it is needed.

In short—we are family.

For many Witches, their coven becomes the family they chose (as opposed to the family they were born into) and takes on a pivotal role in their lives.

So how do you go about finding a group if you decide you want one? If you can't find one, is it okay to just start one? And once you have one, how do you keep it functioning smoothly and working for everyone involved?

Finding a Pagan Group

The first question you need to ask yourself is probably the most important: do you really want to be in a group at all?

I'm not suggesting that it is a bad idea (after all, I love being in Blue Moon Circle), but this isn't a decision to be made lightly. While not all Pagan groups are as closely connected as ours is, most covens involve a fair amount of commitment and interconnectedness. If you are not certain you are ready to commit your time, energy, and focus to other Witches on a long-term basis, you are probably better off limiting your group work to festivals and other such informal gatherings.

So you've made the choice to join a group. Now you need to figure out what kind of group you are looking for. This is less than simple, for two reasons: one, there are almost as many different kinds of Pagan groups as there are Pagans, and two, there may not be any groups of the type you want anywhere near you.

Let's take these issues one at a time.

Generally, groups of Witches are known as covens or circles, and groups of Druids are known as groves, but some Witches use these terms more or less interchangeably. There are also a number of lesser-known terms, usually associated with various specific cultures, like sept and clan (which tend to be used by Celtic Witches). In truth, it doesn't really matter what a group calls itself, as long as the path it follows is one that fits your beliefs and fills your needs.

Among the many different types of Pagan groups, a number can be considered "traditional." This does not mean that only the traditional covens follow the beliefs and practices of previous generations of Witches; in truth, all Witchcraft practiced today is made up of a mixture of the old and the new, and it can be difficult to tell where one starts and the other leaves off.

Traditional covens tend to be those that are based on the teachings of a few early and influential Witches, including Gardnerian (named for founder Gerald Gardner), Alexandrian (for founder Alexander Saunders), Seax-Wica (started by Raymond Buckland), Feri Witchcraft (started by Victor and Cora Anderson), Dianic Witchcraft (which has strong feminist leanings), Reclaiming (co-founded by Starhawk), and Faery Witchcraft (an Irish path).

These covens are usually hierarchical in nature and require their members to work their way through a formal set of teachings, called a degree system. New members must typically study for a year and a day (a common Wiccan time period) to become first-degree initiates, then another year and a day to reach the second level, and again for the third. Eventually, should they continue with the group, most traditional Witches will become either high priests or high priestesses, and "hive off" to form their own covens.

In general, most traditional covens are likely to be somewhat formal in nature, more secretive, and incorporate more ceremonial magick than nontraditional covens. They may insist on robes or other magickal garb, or even work skyclad (that means naked, in case you didn't already know).

There are still traditional covens around, if that is the kind of magickal group you would like to join, but you may have to look a bit harder to find one. Somewhat more common these days is the nontraditional, or Eclectic, coven.

Eclectic covens may be made up of Witches who follow a variety of paths (Blue Moon Circle is one of these) or have members who have agreed not to follow any path in particular. Any given Eclectic group may be made up of Celtic Witches, Green Witches, or assorted other Wiccan/Witch/Pagan folks whose beliefs are close enough that they can practice together. Or an Eclectic coven may follow a particular path, such as Egyptian or Celtic Witchcraft, but not adhere to the formal degree system.

Traditional and Eclectic are only two basic types of Pagan groups; if you are looking hard enough, you can probably find any number of covens and circles that don't fall into either of these categories. It is important to figure out what you are looking for in a group before you join one. Edain McCoy, in her book *The Witch's Coven*, suggests that you make up a "must-haves" list of what you want from a group.

I strongly suggest you make up a list of your own, but here is hers, to give you an idea of what she is talking about:

1. Works robed or in modified street clothing.
2. Has an egalitarian/priestly structure.
3. Expects all members to contribute according to their ability, and all are included in planning sessions.
4. Will accept both Witches who have been initiated by other groups and those who have done self-initiations.
5. Strict substance-free atmosphere.
6. Maintains an outer circle or teaches sincere newcomers.
7. Adheres to a written compact that has been ritually sworn to or signed by all members, and that covers all important aspects of coven life.
8. Views sacred space as safe space for all.
9. Allows for flexible meeting times. (1)

You can see that there are a lot of issues to consider here: how the group members are expected to dress and behave, when a group meets and how often, the degree of acceptance of newcomers, and whether or not there is a degree system are only the tip of the broomstick.

The first group I belonged to, for instance, was also Eclectic, but it was primarily a study group and met every Thursday night, regardless of the phase of the moon or any other considerations. We would occasionally gather on a weekend for a sabbat celebration as well.

In contrast, Blue Moon Circle meets each month for new moons and full moons and gathers for every sabbat. But we are all busy people, with complicated schedules, so some months that means we do a sabbat instead of one of the new moons, or we come together on Wednesday for the full moon that actually fell on the night before.

And we are semi-open in that we will consider new members, but we won't take them unless we feel that they will be a good fit for the group, and we do allow guests at the larger sabbat rituals. Some covens take anyone who asks to be included, others don't allow anyone who isn't in their particular tradition or require a formal trial period before acceptance.

Be sure that whichever group you are considering is flexible enough to accommodate your schedule and focuses on the aspects of Pagan practices that are important to you, without asking you to do anything that makes you feel uncomfortable.

What if you can't find a group that fits all or most of the requirements on your "must-haves" list? Then you have two choices: you can either practice as a Solitary until such time as you find a group that works for you, or you can start your own.

Starting a Pagan Group

Making the decision to join a preexisting group requires a great deal of thought and soul-searching. Choosing to start your own group demands even more of both plus time, energy, and the ability to lead. The rewards can be great, but it is very rarely easy, so be absolutely certain that you are willing to put forth the effort that starting your own coven will entail.

Once you have decided to go ahead, you need to figure out what kind of group you want. Start off with the same wish list you used to look for an existing coven, then add a few things, like how many people you want (here's a hint: start small, then grow when you're ready—Blue Moon Circle consisted of just three of us in the beginning, which enabled us to build a solid foundation for the future) and where you might go looking for them.

If you already know a few people who are interested in starting a group with you, that's probably the easiest path, as long as you all agree on the basics of the group. Sometimes you can put up signs in a local Pagan shop or places that might be Pagan-friendly, like health-food stores and Unitarian churches. Be wary of taking the first people who approach you just so that you can increase your numbers. If they're really not right for the kind of group you have in mind, you are better off waiting for the right folks to come along.

Make sure you are communicating clearly with the other Witches you talk to about forming a group; if possible, come up with a set of written rules (often called a compact) that spell out precisely what is allowed and not allowed, and what you expect from those who become members.

For instance, if you will be requiring attendance at all group rituals, except in the case of emergencies, make sure that people know that ahead of time. If you will want group members to take turns providing cakes and ale, writing rituals, or providing a meeting space, be sure to say that too. Clear communication in the beginning will save you a lot of frustration, hurt feelings, and crushed dreams later on.

Keep in mind that most covens grow and change over time, and what you start out with may not bear much resemblance to what you end up with five or ten years down the road, should your group be lucky enough to stay together that long. Be prepared to be flexible if you want your coven to survive and thrive.

Living with a Pagan Group

Life is full of change; we grow, get new interests, make new friends, and leave old ones behind. Covens are like that too. Very few Pagan groups look the same after they have been in existence for one year, five years, or more.

In truth, many covens don't last that long. It can be hard to keep a bunch of passionate individualists moving in the same direction for extended periods of time. It takes cooperation, flexibility, and, most of all, communication to craft a coven that really works for all of its members, at least most of the time.

Still, plenty of groups have been in existence for a long time, so obviously it can be done. If you want the group you are in to be one of the successful ones, it might help to focus on the three elements I mentioned above: cooperation, flexibility, and communication.

Cooperation

A coven by its very definition is a group that works together toward common goals, both magickal and otherwise. This only works if everyone involved agrees on what those goals are and how to achieve them.

In Pagan groups, this usually comes about in one of two ways. In some covens, the high priest and/or high priestess establishes the basic parameters of how the group will be run, or how magick will be practiced. And then the members of the group follow those rules. In this type of coven, anyone who can't or won't follow the high priest/high priestess's rules will usually be asked to leave, thus preserving the smooth functioning of the group.

In other covens, there may be no specific leader (with members taking turns putting on the rituals) or a high priest/high priestess might lead the group, but all its members create the rules and direction of the coven.

Blue Moon Circle is one of these covens. Much of the leadership of the group falls on my shoulders, in part because I am the only one in the circle who feels comfortable in that role, but I consider myself to be more of a facilitator than the person in charge. All those in the circle have an equal voice, with a little less weight being given to the opinions of those who joined recently and therefore have less invested in the group.

In this sort of coven, it can be more difficult to keep things running smoothly; the more people involved in any decision-making process, the tougher it is to get everyone to agree or play nice with each other. This makes the issue of cooperation even more crucial.

Of course, no matter which kind of coven you are in, group members will need to treat each other with respect, follow whatever rules the group has set up—especially those that protect individual member's privacy, deal with what is and isn't allowed in circle, and dictate when and how new people can be introduced into the group—and act with consideration for the feelings of all those involved.

In Blue Moon Circle, we consider cooperation to include the following:

- Attending all circle activities unless you have an unavoidable conflict or illness (family events, like a child's school concert, are allowed to take precedence, of course).

- Letting me know ahead of time if not attending (since I plan the rituals and do the pre-ritual preparation, it helps to know how many people are coming).

- Keeping the secrets of all other group members—"What is said in circle, stays in circle" is one of our most important rules.

- Not bringing a guest to circle without clearing it with the other group members in advance.

- Allowing all members to have their say, especially when passing the speaking stick.

- Helping each other when necessary—often outside the parameters of formal circle meetings. (We are involved in each other's lives both in and out of circle, which isn't true for all covens; many covens function strictly in the circle setting, and members rarely see each other otherwise. Neither way is right or wrong, it is simply a matter of an individual coven's style.)

- Treating each other with love, respect, and acceptance.

Each Pagan group will have its own definition of cooperation. It is vital that all members follow these rules, whatever they may be.

Sometimes a coven will have one member who is consistently uncooperative and offensive. This can be mildly annoying or it can eventually tear a group apart, depending on how disruptive the behavior is. At the very least, an uncooperative member will throw off the focus of the rest of the circle and make it difficult to create powerful and effective magick.

If you are leading a coven and this type of problem arises, you may have to make a tough decision and ask this person to leave. I suggest that you start by pointing out the problem behavior (in private, not in front of the rest of the group) and asking the individual to change his or her ways. If this doesn't happen in a reasonable amount of time, you may have to bar the uncooperative Witch from attending at all.

For instance, if you are in a group that forbids drinking or drug use during ritual, and one member consistently shows up drunk—a situation I have seen in other covens, unfortunately—that person will destroy the energy you are trying to create in circle and ruin the magickal working for everyone else involved.

In the end, you have to do what is right for the group as a whole. And since cooperation by everyone involved is key to a coven's survival and success, an individual who is unable or unwilling to play by the rules is probably not suited to group work and is better off sticking with a Solitary practice—or possibly, depending on the situation, finding a group with different rules.

Flexibility

This can be a tough one. Most of us resist change, preferring instead to stick with the safe and familiar—even when it isn't working. But just as we need to "go with the flow" in our lives in general, Pagan groups must find ways to roll with the changes that come their way.

When Blue Moon Circle started, it was a very small, intensely focused group. Everyone in it had been practicing some form of Witchcraft, either group or solitary, for many years. Eventually, we expanded somewhat, but the group was still made up primarily of women with a certain amount of experience both in life and in spiritual exploration.

After about four years, though, things gradually shifted. And one day I realized that we had taken on a number of newer members at more or less the same time, and that most of the new additions to the circle were younger or had less Pagan experience, or both. The changes had happened slowly enough that we hadn't noticed or altered the way the group functioned, and the result was that our practice wasn't working as smoothly as it had been.

The long-term members felt as if they were missing the intimate and intense work we'd done as a smaller, more advanced group. The new members weren't getting the in-depth teaching they needed to grow in their Craft and catch up with the rest of us. And I'd started feeling overwhelmed by the increasing demands of managing a larger and more complex group.

This crisis could have gone a number of ways, and believe me, I considered all of them. I could have decided the whole thing was too much to deal with and disbanded the group. Or we could have asked the newer, less experienced members to leave and gone back to our original setup as a smaller circle.

But I didn't want to give up on something that was so important to us all, or penalize the new members simply because they didn't fit into the old format of the group. Still, something fairly drastic had to be done.

So I called the circle together at the next new moon and we had a "where do we go from here" meeting. Everyone was told ahead of time what we would be discussing, so they had a chance to do some serious thinking about what they wanted to get out of being in Blue Moon Circle and how we might go about meeting the needs and desires of everyone involved.

We started out with a prayer for clarity and asked the goddess to guide us to the best new path for the group as a whole. Then we took turns, each lighting a candle and speaking our minds. There was no argument or dissension, no hurt feelings or struggles for power. Just lots and lots of discussion. (And some cookies, of course. It always helps to have cookies.)

In the end, we decided to try completely changing the way the circle worked. While we all agreed that, as Eclectics, we didn't want to follow a traditional hierarchical degree system, it was clear that we needed to address the difference in levels of experience and arcane knowledge. So we decided to try adopting the inner circle/outer circle format used by some other groups.

One of the more experienced Witches volunteered to run the outer circle as sort of an assistant High Priestess. She would lead a teaching circle once a month for the newer members and help them to learn about the rules and ideals that the group was based on, as well as important Witchcraft fundamentals.

On new moons, the inner circle would gather by themselves and return to the smaller, more intense practice we'd all been missing. On full moons and sabbats, the entire circle would come together and practice as equals.

It wasn't a perfect solution, perhaps, but it had the potential to resolve most of the immediate problems we were confronting while still allowing everyone to continue as a member of Blue Moon Circle. And we had come to the decision as a group, in the spirit of perfect love and perfect trust.

All covens will eventually face this challenge or another like it and be required to make changes to accommodate the needs of those who are a part of it. How flexible you are (whether as a leader or a group member) may very well determine the success or failure of that particular group.

I don't recommend staying with a group that no longer meets your needs, but if you like the group you are in, a flexible attitude and a willingness to be open to constructive change can go a long way toward keeping you and your coven practicing magick together happily for years to come.

Communication

Cooperation and flexibility are both important to maintaining a happy and healthy Pagan circle, but neither of them will be of much use if you don't also have good communication.

Communication lets you know what the needs and goals of your group are, which rules you've all agreed to, and the procedure for dealing with problems. It tells you when change is necessary and allows you to come up with the solutions that work best for the group as a whole.

One of the reasons I related the story of Blue Moon Circle's struggle with change was to make exactly this point. Without good communication on the part of everyone involved, this story could have had a much different ending.

I believe that communication is the single most crucial element in successful relationships, whether they are between partners, families, friends, or the members of a Pagan group. If you are the leader of a coven, you have the responsibility to facilitate good communication between all members. If you are a group member, you have the responsibility to speak up in a productive and positive way about those issues that concern you.

Here are a few suggestions for encouraging healthy and effective communication within a coven:

- If communicating as a group, establish sacred space to give everyone a safe place where they feel comfortable opening up and speaking from the heart. If talking to another individual, try to keep distractions to a minimum—choose a time and place where others won't interrupt you, and turn off all phones.

- Make sure that everyone has a chance to speak without interruption. Using a speaking stick, as you would at the end of a ritual, is a great way to achieve this. Pass the stick around the circle; remember that only the person with the stick gets to speak, and all the others should focus their full attention on the one who is talking. No chit-chat should be allowed during this period, and also no interrupting or arguing back. Each person will have a chance to speak his or her mind when the stick gets to them, and it can be sent around the circle more than once if necessary.

- Practice listening. Most of the time, we are all so busy rehearsing what we're going to say in reply, we barely listen when someone else speaks. If your group has real difficulty communicating, try practicing listening and repeating back what someone else has said. When beginning a serious discussion about crucial issues, it is helpful when getting started to gently remind all those taking part to listen when someone else is talking.

- Keep an open mind. If someone brings up a problem or suggests a solution you don't agree with, take a moment to seriously consider what's been said. We are often so attached to our own ideas that it can be hard to make room for someone else's. It's the wise person who's prepared not to get his or her way on all issues and is willing to look for the answers that work for everyone involved.

- Stay calm. There is never a time when open communication is aided by yelling, anger, or accusations. Try to keep your cool. If you're the leader, this is especially crucial. If necessary, ask for a few moments of silence to take a couple of deep breaths, center yourself, and let go of any negative emotions or thoughts. If the discussion starts getting heated or out of control, it is a good idea for the group leader (or someone else, if necessary) to suggest taking a few minutes to ask the gods for help and to focus on working together in perfect love and perfect trust.

- Don't take things personally. Remember that everyone has their issues, especially when interacting with others. Many of these issues stem from our involvement with dysfunctional families or relationships, and they often appear in other social interactions without our conscious intent. Try not to react defensively (even if it seems like someone is attacking you); instead, try responding with calm and loving acceptance. This often defuses a difficult situation without making it worse and allows the other person to back down and regain self-control.

- At the basis of our practice together is the concept of perfect love and perfect trust. It means that we accept each other as we are, warts and all (so to speak). This doesn't necessarily mean that you are going to agree with everyone in your coven all the time. But like a mother with her child, we try to look beyond the surface and love the inner being. After all, if we are each a part of deity, how can we not? And it is hard to have perfect trust, but in truth, if you cannot trust the people in your circle with those things that are the most important, perhaps you shouldn't be practicing with them in the first place.

- When trying to coexist with others in a Pagan group, keep in mind the basic beliefs we all share. Do your best to harm none, and watch your words since they have the power to hurt others. Don't put out anything that you wouldn't be happy to get back in return. Take responsibility for your own actions, and try not to interfere with the free will of others. Do your best to see that spark of divinity in all those around you and to let the light within yourself shine forth. Work together to create positive magick that will benefit you all and the greater world around you.

Something to Try:

If you are considering joining a Pagan group, try making a must-have list of your own. Be as specific as you can, and list everything you can think of that you want in a coven. You will probably not get everything you desire, but at least you will have a clear idea of what you are looking for.

If you are considering starting a Pagan group, you might want to make up a tentative list of rules and goals. Hopefully, you will allow the other members of the coven to have some say about the end result, but your initial list will provide you with a starting point for conversations with those who are interested in joining and allow you to weed out those who are interested in a completely different kind of practice.

If you are currently in a Pagan group that is having difficulties, you might want to make a different sort of list. Try coming up with a pros and cons list: write down all the aspects of the coven that you like and all those that no longer work for you. If possible, come up with suggestions for solutions to the problems and consider discussing them with the leader or leaders of your group or the group as a whole. If you cannot come up with any answers or feel uncomfortable with the idea of talking to people about your issues with the group, this might be a sign that this coven is no longer right for you. You might want to try visualizing your life without the group or the people in it, and see how your heart and the voice of inner wisdom responds.

To explore this topic in greater depth, you may want to read the following book, which is a serious, in-depth study of coven dynamics: *Wicca Covens: How to Start and Organize Your Own* by Judy Harrow.

One final note: never, ever stay in a coven where you are asked to do things that make you uncomfortable. This is especially true for situations that involve sex, drugs of any kind, or any actions that you consider to be against the rule of "harm none." Don't let anyone calling him- or herself a high priest or high priestess override your own ideas of right or wrong. If your inner voice is yelling "Run away!" then do, by all means, listen to it.

....

1   McCoy, *The Witch's Coven*, 23.

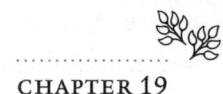

Celebrating the Journey of Life Through Ritual

Daily, Monthly & Yearly

Webster's Dictionary defines "ritual" as "a system of rites, a ceremonial act or action, an act or series of acts regularly repeated in a set precise manner." For Pagans, ritual is all that and more. It can be as simple as looking up at the moon every night or as complex as a Beltane celebration with hundreds of Witches coming from miles around. Some Witches have only formal rituals, performing magick within the confines of a circle and following particular procedures. Others lean more to the informal and are likely to combine their rituals with everyday actions like cooking or gardening.

What are your rituals? Do you have some small act that you do on a daily basis to reconnect with the gods and the universe around you, or are your rituals limited to full moons and sabbats?

There are no rules about how or how often to perform rituals. (Rules? Don't be silly. We're Witches.) I usually suggest that people do some act of ritual at least once a week, and daily if possible. You may believe that you are too busy to be able to fit a ceremony of any kind into an already overloaded life, but I beg to differ. Ritual and ceremony give us the strength to carry on, bring in positive energy, feed the soul, and strengthen our commitment to our own spiritual journey. Surely all that is worth a few minutes a day?

Generally, Pagan rituals tend to fall into three categories: daily, monthly, and yearly. (This doesn't include "special occasion" rites, which we will talk about in the next chapter.) Whether or not you perform any of these will depend in part on your particular path, your schedule, and your own personal inclinations.

Daily Rituals

I will admit that until recently, my own "daily" rituals were a bit sporadic. There were times when I would faithfully go to my altar for a few moments before retiring for the evening, light a candle, and speak a few words to the gods. Sometimes I even managed to do this for two or three weeks in a row before the hustle and bustle of life inevitably got in the way.

Then my circle read a wonderful book by Dianne Sylvan called *The Circle Within: Creating a Wiccan Spiritual Tradition*. In it, she highlights the importance of a personal spiritual practice and building a daily practice to support it. She made a daily practice seem both worthwhile and manageable, and I decided to give it another try.

My first step was to figure out what exactly I wanted to get out of the daily practice. Did I want to practice magick? Perform some specific rite? After I'd pondered the question for a while, I realized that all I really wanted out of a daily ritual was to reinforce my connection with the gods and remind myself regularly of the importance of Witchcraft to my life.

Once I'd determined what it was I wanted, I tried to figure out some routine that I could realistically expect myself to do almost every day. This meant coming up with something that wouldn't get derailed by exhaustion, stress, or a busy schedule.

Oh, sure.

Eventually, I realized that I was taking the term "ritual" too literally. After all, I didn't need to light a candle in order to speak to the gods. I didn't even need to be standing at my altar; I could do it anywhere. And thus my own personal daily practice was born.

It's pretty simple. In the morning, after I wake up but before I open my eyes and get on with my day, I take a few moments to speak to the gods. What

I say to them may change from day to day, but I always start with the same ritual opening words: "Great Goddess, Great God, I come to you at the start of another day and ask that you grant me the best day possible. Help me to feel my best so that I might do my best, for myself and for others."

Depending on what lies ahead of me on any particular day, I may ask for strength, energy, wisdom, prosperity, or any of the other areas where I feel the need of a helping hand. Then I finish up with a ritual closing: "Watch over me and those that I love. So mote it be."

At night, after I have put down my book and turned out the light, I close my eyes and speak again. Now, instead of asking for anything, I take the time to be grateful for all that I have been given. In the evening, I start with different ritual words: "Great Goddess, Great God, I come to you at the end of another day and thank you for all the blessings in my life."

I often give thanks for family, friends, and a job I like. Some days I express gratitude for the gift of creativity or for the strength that got me through a particularly trying experience. What is important is not so much which things I give thanks for, but that I am paying attention to the fact that there are so many things in my life to be grateful for.

This simple daily practice provides me with the connection to deity that I was looking for, and it has the added benefit of reminding me to say please and thank you. My mother would be so proud.

And if you think that maybe I am just lying in bed talking to myself, and not really connecting with the gods, you should know that Magic the cat—who generally tends to ignore me when I speak—always moves from whichever part of the bed she is sprawled upon when I utter those first words and comes to sit by my head until I am done. And she purrs like mad the entire time.

Whether you choose to adopt a ritual like this one or come up with something completely different that's all your own, I hope you will take the time to create a daily practice—or at least a routine you are comfortable doing a few times a week. The gods are with us always, not merely on full moons and holidays, so it is probably a good idea to take a few moments to acknowledge their presence on a regular basis.

Here are a few suggestions for quick, easy, and simple daily rituals:

PRAYER—Prayer doesn't have to be formal or even addressed to any specific god/dess (although if you have one you follow, this is a good way to keep in touch). And if you worry about always asking for something for yourself, you can try praying for the earth. A common and simple prayer like this one is always good: "Let there be peace on earth, and let it begin with me." If you want to get a little more ceremonial about it, you can light a candle on your altar too.

MEDITATION—Meditation is a way to alter your state of consciousness and let go of the issues of the day, if only for a moment. It is good practice for when you want to create a different mental environment for your magickal work, and it can help you learn to better focus. Sit or lie in a comfortable position, and follow the movement of your breath in and out. If you want to make your meditation practice more Pagan-centric, try saying "goddess" with your breath out and "god" with your breath in. Or substitute other words that help you to feel more relaxed and centered, like serenity, oneness, or spirit.

POSITIVE AFFIRMATIONS—It has been scientifically proven that our thoughts influence our physical being (the mind-body connection). In truth, our thoughts influence all aspects of our health: mental, physical, and spiritual. But no one can control his or her thoughts all day long. Instead, try setting aside a few minutes a day to purposely concentrate on the positive. Positive affirmations are short statements that are aimed at changing our negative physical or emotional patterns by replacing them with more beneficial ones. They are always voiced in the present tense. For instance, if you are struggling with trying to lose weight, your positive affirmation might be "I am eating healthier and am satisfied with smaller portions." Because I have ongoing health issues, one of my favorite affirmations is "I am strong and healthy; my body is balanced and working perfectly." Positive affirmations can be combined with meditation or even exercise.

YOGA/TAI CHI/QI GUNG—These are all forms of exercise that are designed to be spiritual as well as physical. When they are done slowly and mindfully, yoga and tai chi can leave you feeling more centered and more grounded.

Qi gung (Chi Kung, Qigong) helps to move your energy, or qi (chi), through your body. And these exercises also strengthen your body as they refresh your spirit. Many people who practice yoga on a regular basis like to start their day with what is called the "Sun Salutation," a series of movements that flow smoothly from one yoga pose to another as you greet the new day. What could be more Pagan than saluting the sun?

AURA CLEANSING—This is a good one to do at the end of the day, before you go to bed or when you come home from work (especially if you work in a physically or psychically toxic environment). The intention is to get rid of whatever negativity you have picked up during the course of the day. One easy way to do this is to leave a bowl of water by the front door. Whenever you come in, take a moment to focus on sending anything icky into the water. If you do this for a while, you will probably notice the water turning cloudy or darker, so it is a good idea to replace it periodically with a fresh bowl. Alternately, you can use incense or a sage smudge stick to clean your aura, or even just envision yourself surrounded by a glowing, positive light.

READ—There are a number of good books available that contain one-a-day spells, rituals, meditations, or Pagan-oriented readings. Try reading a page every day from one of the following: *Pagan Every Day* by Barbara Ardinger, *The Real Witches' Year* by Kate West, or *Llewellyn's Spell-A-Day Almanac* (put out yearly).

Monthly Rituals

Almost all Witches observe the full moon in one way or another, and some also include the new moon as well. It is traditional for Pagan practices to center around the moon and her changing outline, which so visibly represents the ebb and flow of our own lives. For many of us, the moon is a symbol of the goddess herself, and we follow her journey across the sky as she follows our journey here on earth.

Of course, you don't have to limit your monthly practice to the moon. Some Witches see the sun as a symbol of the god and incorporate sun rituals into their routine as well.

Unlike a daily practice, in which the rituals are more likely to be spiritual than magickal in nature, monthly rituals tend to be a mixture of both. If you are in a coven, you may gather for study at the new moons and work spells on the full moons. As a Solitary, you may not even observe the new moon at all. And if that is the case, you may be missing out on a surprisingly powerful time for ritual work.

Traditionally, there are two views regarding the best way to use the energy of the new moon. One is to see it as the first day of the waxing cycle of the moon and therefore a time for doing spellwork that will tap into the increasing energy of the moon as she grows ever rounder in the sky above. The second is to see it as a quiet time; a short space of rest and lack of movement best suited for internal exploration and the pause that comes before new efforts are put into motion.

I agree with both these theories.

I know; it seems like you would have to pick one or the other, but need I remind you that we are Witches, and we make our own rules?

My suggestion is that you use the new moon for whichever purpose most suits your needs in any particular month, and tap into your intuition to get a feel for what will work best with the energies of that specific moon.

I have found that some months, the new moon energy seems to want to be used for quiet activities, and at other times it seems like the perfect point at which to start a magickal working that will continue on throughout the rest of the waxing moon's cycle. I don't know if the difference is actually in the moon or if it is coming from something internal to my own desires—and honestly, I don't know that it matters.

Much of the power of our magickal practice is generated by our ability to connect with our own intuitive wisdom, and that is true for your new moon rituals as well. But if you are having a hard time coming up with rituals for the new moon, help is as close as the nearest Pagan bookstore. *Rituals of the Dark Moon: 13 Lunar Rites for a Magical Path* contains a year's worth of inspirational and powerful rituals designed especially for use on the dark moon, the night before the new moon.

Author Gail Wood shares a journey into the dark and mysterious side of the moon, with thirteen rituals created using the energies of the zodiac signs of each month's moon. For instance, there is "The Unseen in Aquarius," "Intuition in Scorpio," and "Creativity in Sagittarius." Together, the rituals in this book provide a great springboard for an exploration into the lesser-known dark moon rituals.

Of course, you can also come up with your own rituals, or simply use the time of the new moon or dark moon to sit in silence and commune with the goddess.

The full moon, on the other hand, has a more obvious and potent energy. Who hasn't been aware of the eerie glow of the full moon hanging high up in the sky on a clear winter night? Or felt the urge to kick off their shoes and run howling through the summer grass?

Women are especially sensitive to the pull of the moon, which is so intertwined with our own monthly cycles. I always find I have trouble sleeping for a few nights before, during, and after the full moon. Even with the blinds closed, I can sense her presence.

So why not make the most of this powerful night? If you need help with some area of your life, whether it is your health, your finances, or your love life, now is the time to cast a spell to put your intent out into the universe. Or light a candle and meditate on a troubling question so that the moon can shine her light on the answers.

Another good book that focuses on the moon in her many phases is *Everyday Moon Magic: Spells & Rituals for Abundant Living* by Dorothy Morrison. A comprehensive overview of lunar magick, this book also includes circle ideas and moon party suggestions for every month, for those who work in a group.

Unlike a daily ritual, which is likely to be more or less the same all the time, your monthly ritual practice will probably change throughout the course of the year. Some months it may focus on your internal journey, while in others it will be all about your external goals. But even during those months that find you too busy for formal ritual or too unfocused for profound inner wisdom to find its way to the surface, be sure to take a moment to light a candle on your altar or stand outside and greet our Lady Moon with a cheerful "Merry meet!"

If you don't feel the inclination to center your practice around the moon (and not everyone does), or if you want something extra to do in addition to any lunar ceremonies you already have in your schedule, you can try integrating one or more of these into your monthly rituals:

PROSPERITY MAGICK—Perform before paying bills, balancing your checkbook, taking your paycheck to the bank, big grocery shopping, or any other monthly tasks that involve money (and yes, I suppose that includes playing the lottery, if you do so). This can be as simple as lighting a green candle, dabbing your wallet with some prosperity oil, and asking for help with the math. Or you can do a full-on ritual, complete with circle casting and spells.

HEALING MAGICK—Perform before going to the doctor, the dentist, or the vet, or on a regular basis if you have ongoing health issues. For instance, if you have problems that tend to crop up once a month (and ladies, you know what I'm talking about here), you can do magick to ease pain or bring serenity.

LOVE MAGICK—Perform before a special evening with your honey, should you be fortunate enough to have one, or before going out to a social event, if you don't. Remember, the trick with love magick is to make sure that you aren't interfering with anyone else's free will. But there's no reason why you can't do a spell to ask for passion, enjoyment, or confidence for yourself. If you are one of the busy moms or dads who rarely gets the chance to have sex with your significant other, you can do a little love magick to make those occasions even more extraordinary.

PROTECTION MAGICK—Try integrating this into a few of your regular chores, like washing your car, checking the air in the tires, mowing the lawn, cleaning out your chimney, or backing up your computer. If you live in the city and regularly use public transportation, you may want to do protection magick once a month over your bus pass or subway tokens.

MENTAL SHARPNESS MAGICK—This includes magick for creativity, focus, wisdom, and such. You could do this before any big project that requires you to be especially brilliant, or even before taking your child to the library. If you are in school, it can be particularly helpful before a big test.

PSYCHIC MAGICK—Try doing some form of prediction magick or practice every month using whichever tool you prefer. Once or twice a month, check in with your future by doing a tarot reading, pulling out a few runes, or sleeping with a dream sachet tucked under your pillow for a night or two. You don't have to ask a specific question for this ritual, just a general "what do I need to know for the month ahead" will do.

Yearly Rituals

Most Pagans follow a yearly calendar of holidays commonly referred to as the Wheel of the Year. Unlike the esbats, or full moons, which are most often used for magick or study, the eight sabbats of the Pagan year are primarily times for celebration.

This is not to say that Witches don't do magickal work on the sabbats; of course they do. But the sabbats are also holidays, many of them following traditions passed down from ancient Pagan practices that celebrated the changing seasons and their connection with the earth.

There are eight holidays in the Wheel of the Year: two solstices, two equinoxes, and four cross-quarter holidays that fall in between. The esbats focus on the moon, but the sabbats follow the path of the sun and the greater celestial movement of the earth itself. In addition, the Wheel of the Year tells the story of the god and the goddess as they change with the seasons. As with most mythology, there are variations in the tale, depending on who does the telling, but the basics are generally accepted by most of the Pagan community.

Samhain

Also known as the Witches' New Year, Samhain is at once the end of one year and the beginning of another. Probably the most profoundly witchy of all the sabbats, Samhain is the origin of the holiday that is famous for Witches and ghosts and things that go bump in the night: Halloween.

On October 31, Witches gather to mourn those whom they have lost and to speak to their ancestors. It is said that the veil between the worlds of the living and the dead is at its thinnest on this night, which is probably where Halloween got its spooky reputation. But for Witches, it is also a time of joyous celebration—the start of a new year in which anything is possible.

Most Samhain rituals involve a bonfire, candles, and incense, and take place after dark. Blue Moon Circle tries to celebrate this holiday outside, no matter how cold it is. (You can always put on long johns underneath your cool black dress, and this is a great time to pull out that hooded cloak that's been hiding in the back of your closet.) The smell of the fire, the sound of the crackling wood, and the quiet chanting of a circle of Witches makes for a truly moving experience.

Samhain honors the goddess in her guise as Crone. The god is absent, resting in the belly of his mother, waiting to be reborn at Yule. (And, yes, it seems contradictory that the goddess is both Mother and Crone at the same time. Welcome to the wonderful world of Wicca.)

Samhain can be observed alone in silence or shared with a large group. No matter what form of ritual you use on this most witchy of holidays, be sure to honor your ancestors, say any goodbyes that remain to be said, and open your heart to the possibilities of the year to come.

A SIMPLE SAMHAIN RITUAL—Take a bowl (or cauldron) and fill it with sand (or course salt). Place a number of tealights or small taper candles in the bowl, then put it where you can sit comfortably in front of it. Sit quietly for a while, and let the silence of the night seep into your soul. As you sit, think about all the people who contributed to making you who you are today. Light a candle for your ancestors, parents, teachers, friends—anyone who has helped to shape the clay that is the essence of you. Say goodbye to any who have gone on to the next part of their journey, and listen carefully in case they have any last words of advice.

Yule

This sabbat is also known as the Winter Solstice, and it is the origin of many of the traditions now associated with Christmas. Yule celebrates the beginning of the return of the light and the eventual end of winter. Although it may seem odd to be looking ahead to the end of the season that is just starting, the Winter Solstice marks the point where each day there is a little more light and a little less dark.

The night of the solstice itself is the longest night of the year; perhaps our Pagan ancestors felt the need to create light against the darkness. On this night, it is traditional to light many candles, and evergreen wreaths or trees are used to symbolize the green of life when so much else of nature is either dead or sleeping.

The goddess, as Mother, gives birth to the infant god as part of the cycle of birth, growth, death, and rebirth. And so hope is born again, bringing warmth and light out of the cold and darkness.

> A SIMPLE YULE RITUAL—Place candles on fire-safe surfaces through-out your home or apartment; keep one taper and some matches near you. Turn out the lights, and feel the dark of winter surround you like a comfortable velvet cloak. Then light your taper and walk around the house, lighting the rest of the candles off it. As each candle adds to the brightness in your home, feel the love and light of the goddess filling your spirit.

Imbolc

One of the cross-quarter holidays, Imbolc falls at the beginning of February and is the origin of the secular holiday now known as Groundhog Day. At this time of the year, many of us are looking out the window at piles of snow and hanging icicles. Nevertheless, Imbolc celebrates the first stirrings of spring, even if we cannot see them.

Change is in the air; the goddess returns to her form as Maiden, and the god is slowly growing from an infant into a sturdy child. It is time for us to start thinking about change as well. Pagans often use this holiday for cleansing and purification and to begin looking ahead to the path that we will follow in the year to come.

A SIMPLE IMBOLC RITUAL—Take a number of small slips of paper and write on each one a word or phrase that can be used for guidance on your path. (For example: patience, courage, new beginnings, take a leap of faith, let go, prosperity, and so forth.) Fold each slip in half so that you can't peek at what is written on it, and put them all in a small bowl. Set the bowl and a single white candle on a table, and settle yourself comfortably in front of them. Ask the gods to send you guidance and inspiration to help you in the year to come.

Gaze at the candle and feel its small warmth hint at spring's possibilities. Think about any questions you might have about the paths that lie ahead of you. When you are ready, reach inside the bowl and pull out a slip of paper. Look at the word or words on the paper you picked, and think about what they might mean for your journey.

Spring Equinox

Who doesn't want to celebrate spring? Okay, it's true that where I live, in the snowy Northeast, we are just as likely to have snow for Spring Equinox as we are for Imbolc, but a Witch can dream, can't she?

Also known as Ostara, after the goddess Eostre, this holiday is the origin of many of the traditions now known for being associated with Easter. Ironically, Ostara is a fertility holiday, which celebrates the resurgence of life with such symbols as rabbits and cute little chicks.

The equinox is a time of balance, when there is an equal amount of light and dark. The only other day this happens all year is on the Autumn Equinox. From now until then, there will be more light than there is darkness, and growth will reign triumphant over death.

The goddess is the Maiden in all her youthful glory, the god is reaching manhood, and energy abounds. Why not tap into that energy to bring the light into your own darkness, if you have any? This is the perfect time of year to clear away all those old patterns that no longer work for your benefit, and welcome in new growth, whether spiritual, personal, or financial.

A SIMPLE SPRING EQUINOX RITUAL—Buy a few bulbs or a packet of seeds. Anything colorful and exuberant will do; if it is something that can be used for magick later, that's a bonus, but it is not absolutely necessary. Take the slip of paper you pulled out at Imbolc if you did that ritual, or create a new piece specifically for this ritual. Write down the things you want to blossom and grow over the coming season. (Love? Prosperity? A new career? All of the above? It's up to you. These are your wishes, after all. Don't worry about whether or not they are likely or even possible. Just wish.) Then take a small pot or cauldron and plant your seeds and your wishes together. Be sure to give them lots of good energy to help them grow!

Beltane

Probably the most important Pagan holiday after Samhain (or at least the most popular), Beltane is based on an ancient Celtic fire festival. And the passion of fire is definitely in the air. May Day, as it is also known, is a holiday that celebrates life and fertility.

This day is all about passion. The goddess and the god are joined in an amorous marriage, and the land bursts back into life as the outward expression of their love and joy. Beltane is a wonderful time to celebrate with other Witches, if you can; dancing, singing, and drumming in honor of the gods and of life itself.

This holiday is the perfect time for love spells and for magick dealing with increase of any kind. If you can't gather with other Pagans, try this ritual instead.

A SIMPLE BELTANE RITUAL—Why not create a ritual that celebrates the sensual? This doesn't necessarily have to have anything to do with sex (although if you're lucky enough to have a partner, you can share this ritual with him or her). Indulge your senses. Put sweet-smelling flowers on the altar, eat some chocolate or a decadent desert. Put on whatever music touches your soul, and dance for joy at the Lady and Lord's wedding. Smooth on a little massage oil—or have someone else do it for you—and celebrate the simple pleasures of being alive.

Summer Solstice

Midsummer! Also known as Litha, this solstice holiday is the longest day of the year and the shortest night. The earth is at its most fertile, and life is bursting out all over (yes, even here in the Northeast).

The goddess, in her role as Mother, is pregnant with the child of her consort, the sun god, and the whole world blooms with her. This is the best time for magickal work for abundance, fertility, and any kind of growth. If you can, try to celebrate outside amidst the glorious outpouring of nature's glory.

> A SIMPLE SUMMER SOLSTICE RITUAL—At this time, when the earth's gifts are so openly displayed, take the opportunity to give back a little. Instead of a complicated ritual, why not plant a tree for your Mother? If you have a place of your own, you can plant one of the traditional witchy trees like oak or willow. If you don't have room to keep a tree, donate one to a local park, or send money to the Arbor Day Foundation and plant something small at home to symbolize your gift. Take a moment to give thanks for all the gifts of the land—and be sure to clean up after yourself. After all, your Mother is watching.

Lammas

Lammas is another cross-quarter day, the first of three Pagan harvest festivals. The harvest was a very important part of early Pagan life—literally a matter of life and death. You can see why three of the eight holidays in the Witches' year revolve around the celebration of food and fellowship.

Also known as Lughnasadh in honor of Lugh, the Celtic god of light, Lammas is a celebration of grain and the beginning of the summer harvest season. In some traditions, this is also a time of sadness, when the god willingly sacrifices himself to ensure the continued fertility of the land. (In other traditions, this doesn't happen until the Autumn Equinox.) But he lives on in the form of the goddess's unborn child and so represents the continuing cycle of life, growth, death, and rebirth.

This holiday is often celebrated with the symbolic sacrifice of a corn dolly or the ritual sharing of bread. Now is also the time to rejoice at our personal harvests and give thanks for our mental, physical, and spiritual gains of the past year. We begin to see the fruits of our labors and decide how we can best apply the energy of what we've reaped.

> A SIMPLE LAMMAS RITUAL—Since bread is a traditional symbol of this holiday, bake some for yourself. You don't have to be a master baker—there are plenty of mixes available if you don't want to start from scratch. This is a little bit of kitchen magick. While you are mixing your ingredients, concentrate on the things you wish to harvest over the next few months. Mix in your wishes and hopes, your yearnings and your dreams. (And maybe an egg.) When your bread is done, sit at your altar and slowly eat a slice dripping with butter or jam. Or share your bread—and all your good wishes—with your family and friends.

Autumn Equinox

Where I live, the Autumn Equinox brings with it a hint of the winter to come. The days are still warm and beautiful, but the nights have a chilly edge, and the leaves are beginning to change colors and fall to the ground.

The Autumn Equinox, also known as Mabon, is the second day in the year when the light and dark are in perfect balance. We stand poised on the brink of the darker half of the year, torn between the desire to celebrate the sun and the heavily pregnant goddess and the need to start storing food and energy away against the dark, cold times to come.

This is the second Pagan harvest festival, often observed with foods like corn, squash, and apples as they hit their peak in the growing cycle. We raise a glass of cider in honor of the god's sacrifice and give thanks for the bounty of the harvest. Mabon is also known as "the Witches' Thanksgiving," and it is now, more than ever, that we take time out to thank the earth for all of her gifts and the gods for watching over us as we tread the Wheel of the Year.

> A SIMPLE AUTUMN EQUINOX RITUAL—Light a candle outside under a starry sky, or sit at a bonfire if you have a place for one. On a piece of paper or in your head, list all of the aspects of your life for which you are grateful. Thank the gods out loud for all their gifts. Then think about the things that no longer work for you. What stands in the way of your personal harvest? Resolve to sacrifice it so that the rest of your life might

prosper. If you can, write it down, and burn it in the fire. Then sit and enjoy the autumn night, and perhaps come up with a few ideas of how to best use the cold, dark days ahead.

No matter how you celebrate the sabbats—alone or with others, inside or outside, with complicated spells or simple, heartfelt meditation—take the time on these eight days to connect with your Pagan past and the wide-open possibilities of your magickal future. Ritual helps us to put our lives into context and make them concrete and solid, and unites us with each other, if only in spirit.

And what about the other holidays in the year, the ones that can be found on the mundane calendar? If you want, you can put a Pagan spin on those as well. Here are a few ideas to try:

NEW YEAR'S EVE—Witches have their own New Year's at Samhain, but that can be a fairly somber holiday. So when the "official" New Year rolls around, you might as well celebrate all over again. Try doing a ritual for new beginnings, and write down a list of all the dreams that you would like to manifest in the year to come. Then burn your list in a bonfire so that the ashes will float your wishes up to the gods, or stick it in your underwear drawer, so that every time you open it, you are reminded of your goals for the year.

MARTIN LUTHER KING DAY—Take a few moments to thank the gods that we live in a time when Witches are (reasonably) free to live as we please, and send out a prayer for all those around the globe who still deal with oppression and prejudice.

GROUNDHOG DAY—Most of us are celebrating Imbolc at this time, but if you aren't going to do a ritual for the Pagan holiday, try doing a "look for your own shadow" ritual for the mundane one. We all have aspects of ourselves that we would rather not look at too closely, and these are usually the things that stand in the way of our leading the happiest and most productive lives possible. Cast a protective circle and do some cleansing work to start. Then light a white candle and place it in front of a mirror. Center yourself, and feel the goddess's love surround you. When you're ready, spend some time looking into the mirror, or meditate to look inside with your inner sight. Be sure to have compassion for yourself, no matter what you find there. Then resolve to bring that shadow into the light of day, and blow out the candle.

VALENTINE'S DAY—Obviously, this is a good day for love or sex magick. (Woo hoo!) If you have someone to share the day with, whip up a little love magick in the kitchen. Make a batch of cupcakes (chocolate, of course); they don't have to be from scratch if you're short of time or baking-impaired. Add any of the edible plants that are good for love magick: rose petals, lavender, or orange peel are all good for this. Once they're cooked, you can decorate the tops with symbols drawn in frosting, such as hearts, pentacles, or runes like Gifu (for gifts and generosity), Ansuz (for communication and harmony), or Fehu (for fulfillment). Remember to imbue them with your feelings of love and passion with every step.

ST. PATRICK'S DAY—Okay, this is a tough one. St. Patrick was definitely *not* a patron saint of Witches. In fact, when they talk about St. Patrick driving the snakes out of Ireland, it is actually a reference to him driving Pagans out of the country. (Boo, hiss.) So you might want to use this day to do some snaky magick in return. Snakes are a Pagan symbol of change and regeneration because of the way they shed their skins and tunnel into and out of the ground. You don't have to be a big fan of reptiles in their real live slithery forms to do this ritual, although if you happen to own a snake, you can bring it into circle to help you out. All you need for this ritual is a sheet, a cloak, or any large piece of cloth. Cast a circle, and listen to some snake-charming music for a while. Think about shedding your own skin and reinventing yourself with a new exterior, maybe one that is stronger, or more beautiful, or more creative. Let the music carry you into an altered state of mind, then get down on the floor and slither yourself under the sheet. Stay there until you feel yourself changing, then slither out the other side and back into your life.

EASTER—Not our holiday, that's for sure. But why not have fun with the Pagan symbols the Christians have adopted as their own for this day? Color eggs (then decorate them with Pagan symbols), eat chocolate rabbits, and celebrate the theme of this holiday: rebirth and resurrection. If you want to get serious about it, you can try doing some past-life regression to find out who you were in your last life. If you'd rather take a more lighthearted approach, resurrect a favorite item of furniture or clothing by adding patches, some dye, or a new paint job.

EARTH DAY—Man, is this our holiday or *what*? There are all kinds of ways that you can celebrate this important day. Go out and clean up the earth a bit by picking a section of a local park, river, or highway to rid of trash and debris. Or plant a tree, a bush, or anything else that will help to generate oxygen and help clean the air. Spend the day in appreciation of all the gifts that the earth gives us: food, water, and a place to live, to name a few. This is the perfect day to do a healing ritual for the earth. And don't forget to get outside and enjoy the planet.

MOTHER'S DAY—Pagans are big on mothers, so be sure to do something nice for yours today. Chocolate is nice, of course, but how about something a little more meaningful? Write a poem or a card in your own words that tells her how much you appreciate her. Say thank you for all the things she has done for you, and be specific so she knows that you were really paying attention. If you want to be a mother and it hasn't happened yet, perhaps do some fertility magick to help things on their way.

MEMORIAL DAY—I have a tough time with this holiday, because I am very much anti-war and anti-violence. On the other hand, I respect those who have sacrificed to keep this country safe. Memorial Day is a good time to say thank you to all those who gave their lives in service of others: soldiers, firemen (and women), policemen (and women), and the like. Take a moment on this day to light a candle in appreciation of those who take on the difficult and dangerous tasks necessary to keep a society functioning. Perhaps also send out blessings to all those who are currently risking their lives on our behalf, and ask the gods to keep them safe. If you want to go that extra mile, you can send a card to a Pagan soldier or two, to let them know that they are not forgotten.

FATHER'S DAY—Remember that Pagans are equal-opportunity worshippers: we appreciate our father/god as much as we do our mother/goddess. So let's make sure that we celebrate the father's role as much as we do the mother's, especially in this day and age when many fathers are raising their children alone. Whatever you did to show your appreciation to Mom will probably work for Dad (he likes chocolate too, you know). And don't forget that Pagans often have rather flexible gender roles. If you know a woman who feels more like a father than a mother, you can celebrate her on this day, and the same goes for any male that takes on a mother role.

INDEPENDENCE DAY—The Fourth of July is a day to celebrate the fact that we won the war that determined our independence as a country, so use this day to celebrate your own independence. What wars have you fought and won? Have you triumphed over addiction or bad habits? Are you transitioning from childhood to adulthood or leaving a bad relationship to stand on your own two feet? This is a good time to do a ritual that reinforces your own personal strengths and moves you one step closer to achieving your goals.

LABOR DAY—This holiday is all about work and an appreciation for those who labor to make our world a better place, which makes it the perfect day to do any work-related rituals. If you are looking for a new job, want to improve the one you have, or want to convince your boss to give you a raise, this is the day to do that magickal rite. Be sure to focus on the positive, then take a little time to be grateful for whatever work you do.

COLUMBUS DAY—In theory, this day celebrates the fact that Christopher Columbus discovered the New World. In reality, this turns out to be a point of some contention. There are some who believe that the Vikings, in particular Leif Ericson, found America first. Still others point out that since there were actually people living here at the time (the folks we now call Native Americans), it was less a matter of "discovering" than it was a matter of "coming in and taking over." It's not much of a reason to have a holiday when viewed in that light. So instead of looking at the man, or at all the baggage his three little ships carried with them, let's look at the spirit of exploration that is really at the heart of this holiday. You don't have to sail the ocean blue in search of glory and adventure, either. Just dedicate this day to some form of exploration, whether that means driving down a road a mile from your house that you just never happened to take before, embarking on a spiritual journey, or even exploring those old boxes your grandmother tucked into a corner of the attic. Allow yourself to take a small leap into the unknown, and see what mysteries await you there. After all, a whole new world lies outside your door, if only you take the time and effort to explore it.

HALLOWEEN—Obviously, this is also Samhain, and most of us will do some sort of ritual for the sabbat. But what if you find yourself—because of friends or children—celebrating the more mundane side of this holiday too? If you can, try dressing up as somebody or something completely different from your everyday self. We all love putting on our garb and letting our witchy side show through, but how about taking this opportunity to reflect some other facet of your personality? Find a costume that is nothing like the face you normally let the world see: if you are independent, try dressing as a slave girl; if you are modest, wear something wild and provocative. Let your hidden self come out and play, and see what happens when you step outside your comfort zone. You may surprise yourself, and you will almost certainly surprise everybody else.

THANKSGIVING—This one is a no-brainer. Take the day to do a ritual of thanks, and send out appreciation for all the blessings in your life. Celebrate the family and friends (furry and two-legged) who share the day with you. If you don't have a big family dinner planned, you may want to volunteer to help serve at a community meal for the poor or elderly. There is nothing like seeing others who have less than you to make you appreciate what you've got, even if you don't feel like your life is all that blessed most of the time.

CHRISTMAS—I know, this one's not our holiday either. But many folks grew up celebrating it and don't want to give it up altogether or are still part of a family that observes the traditional Christian holidays. And most of us have friends and coworkers for whom Christmas is a pretty big deal. The great thing about this holiday is that so many of its customs are similar to Pagan traditions, it is easy to have a party that includes elements of both Christmas and Yule. And yes, I realize that a party is not the same thing as a ritual, but you can do a ritual beforehand, and ask for "peace on earth and goodwill toward humanity," and then bring that positive energy into your celebration with those you love.

Don't forget to integrate your magickal practice with your own personal yearly holidays: birthdays, anniversaries, and the like. On your birthday, you can do a ritual in which you outline all the things you'd like to achieve during the next year or focus on one goal to be attained before your next birthday. Or you can do an annual "rebirthing" of yourself, and start every new year refreshed and rejuvenated. One easy way to do this is to run a bath, add some magickal oils for cleansing and purification (bubble bath optional), and soak in it until your skin is as wrinkled as it was the first time you were born. You can even use chocolate soap if you're feeling particularly decadent.

For an anniversary ritual, you can do something together if your sweetie is Pagan or open to Pagan practices. Otherwise, you can certainly do a ritual by yourself and still have it be effective. Try doing some magick for communication or patience, if things aren't going smoothly. Or come up with a yearly ritual for the two of you that isn't necessarily an obvious form of magick; after all, ritual isn't limited to spells and incantations, and a yearly formal dinner where you both dress up to the nines and treat each other like lovers can be pretty darn magickal even without anything "extra" thrown in.

Any occasion that only comes around once a year can be turned into a part of your spiritual practice, but there are also yearly maintenance rituals that are simply a good idea. For instance, you might want to set aside a day every year to renew the protection charms or blessings on your house, apartment, or car (sometime in the spring is good for this; use the change to daylight savings time to remind you, if you like). I try to do a ritual cleansing of my altar at least once a year too.

It doesn't really matter which, if any, of these suggestions you choose to follow. What matters is that you do whatever feels right to you to make your spiritual beliefs an integral part of your everyday life. By adding in daily, monthly, and yearly rituals, you will be ensuring that you regularly reconnect with your gods, your spirit, and your intention as an Everyday Witch.

Something to Think About:

What do you want out of a daily practice? What is the best way to fit one into your life? Write down all the aspects of your ideal daily practice, then figure out a practical way to apply at least the most important aspects to a form of ritual that you will actually do.

Something to Try:

Here are two more books I recommend, both of which feature a year of ritual or celebration. They are very different from each other, covering various aspects of Pagan and witchy practice and tradition.

Ceremonies of the Seasons: Exploring and Celebrating Nature's Eternal Cycle by Jennifer Cole

A Year of Ritual: Sabbats and Esbats for Solitaries & Covens by Sandra Kynes

And here are some other books that have some form of spell or ritual for every day:

Pagan Every Day: Finding the Extraordinary in Our Ordinary Lives by Barbara Ardinger

The Llewellyn Spell-A-Day Almanac (released yearly)

365 Goddesses by Patricia Telesco

The Real Witches' Year: Spells, Rituals and Meditations for Every Day of the Year by Kate West

And don't forget to check out my first book, if you haven't already:

Circle, Coven & Grove: A Year of Magickal Practice

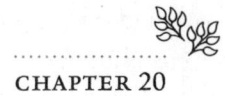

Rites of Passage

Birth, Coming of Age, Marriage, Eldering, and Passing Over

In addition to the rituals we use in our daily lives or on a regular basis as we follow the esbat and sabbat cycle throughout the year, there are a number of rituals that we use on rare occasions to celebrate special events. Some of these occasions are happy ones, like the birth of a child or a wedding. Others may be sad or bittersweet.

Ritual, whether practiced on our own or with others, can mark the most important moments of our existence and help us either cope or celebrate, depending on the circumstances. There are any number of experiences over the course of a life well-lived that are worthy of a formal ceremony; the ones listed here are just a few of the most common.

Birth

One traditional way to celebrate the birth of a Witch's baby is called a Wiccaning. Unlike a christening, which dedicates the newborn to the religion of his parents, a Wiccaning is simply a ceremony to welcome a child into the Pagan community and introduce him or her to the gods.

As Witches, we believe that each individual must make his or her own choice about a spiritual path, so we wouldn't tie a small child to our own Pagan belief system. He or she will have time enough to make that choice later. Instead, we gather together—either on a family level, as a coven, or in a larger community setting—and greet the child as he or she embarks on the journey of life.

I have been to such rituals, and they can be truly moving occasions. Often, mother and child sit in the middle of the circle, and the child is presented to the community. Then the members of the child's extended family (sometimes everyone there) come up one at a time and present the child with a gift. Sometimes there is an actual gift, usually a token of the spiritual wishes that the giver bestows. One person might give the gift of wisdom, for instance, while another offers the hope of good health.

During this ceremony, the child is formally granted the protection of the gods and the community. This does not mean that these things are not available to all Pagan children, with or without a Wiccaning—this is simply a ritual to acknowledge that fact. At the core of this ritual is all the love and positive energy that is offered to the newest member of the community and the pledges by those who will stand in for the child's parents should there be a need for extra help or guidance.

Blue Moon Circle also celebrates the birth of a circle-sister's child by doing a "safe childbirth" spell for mother and child on the full moon before the delivery. This spell can be done at any time in the days leading up to the birth, and it can be done by an individual just as easily as by a group.

The benefit of having a group perform the spell is that there will be a number of people focusing their energy on the goal, but one Witch with a fervent wish in her heart can certainly cast this spell to good effect. Just remember never to do this spell on a pregnant woman without her permission. (Even when carrying a new life, one is entitled to free will. Once the child is born, of course, all bets are off. Mothers of infants rarely get to be in control of anything.)

When Blue Moon Circle performs this spell, we don't use any bells or whistles. We simply gather in a sacred circle, put the mom-to-be in the middle, and recite the spell while directing the energy of our love and hope toward her and her child.

If you wanted to do something more ornate, you certainly could, especially if you are doing the spell alone, without a group.

To raise more energy, you could clip out lots of pictures of healthy babies and moms and put them on an altar or table. If you know the gender of the baby, you could use a blue candle for a boy or a pink candle for a girl—otherwise, yellow or white is fine. Anoint the candle with the healing or good fortune oil of your choice (heather or orange would be good), and place a vase of flowers at the pregnant woman's feet. You can use daisies for positive outcome or rose buds that haven't fully blossomed to symbolize the mom herself.

If you have any particular gifts to give her or the baby, you can do that now. (I can tell you from experience that new moms really appreciate coupons for an hour of housecleaning, a meal she doesn't have to cook, or a movie's worth of babysitting.)

Then light the candle while concentrating on all your good wishes for mom and child, visualize her surrounded by a protective white light, and recite the following spell (*note*: if it is just you and the mom-to-be, she can recite the spell with you):

Childbirth Spell

Women by nature, Witches by choice
We speak together with a single voice
To pool our power, to work our will
We ask the goddess this wish fulfill
Aid this woman in childbirth's bed
Cut through pain, leave joy instead
Healthy mother, healthy child
Labor that is short and mild
Birth as a blessing, come when it may
Guard this woman on her labor day
So mote it be

Coming of Age

Most ancient cultures had rituals to acknowledge the coming of age of their children. Unfortunately, this is a tradition that has been abandoned by modern society, and our youth often seem lost in a wasteland between childhood and adulthood.

Pagans recognize that this transition is an important one, and many Witches are now incorporating some kind of coming of age ritual into the lives of their children. Again, this is not a ritual that binds the teen to a religious path; rather, it is the recognition that they have reached an age where they will start making decisions on their own and bear the bulk of the responsibility for their own actions.

Coming of age rituals can take place at various times. Some children are honored when they reach sexual maturity: when a girl has her first menstrual period or when a boy shows outward signs of sexual maturity such as hair growth or a lower voice. Others choose to have a ritual at a certain age, such as thirteen or eighteen, or when a child goes off to college or leaves the parent's home to live on his or her own.

The timing of a coming of age ritual depends a great deal on the individual—all children mature at different rates, and some parents are ready to let go earlier than others. If you are planning to have a coming of age ritual for your child, make sure that you both feel that the time is right. Sometimes a Pagan parent will suggest to the child that a ritual would be appropriate, and sometimes a teen will ask for the rite themselves. Either way, the ceremony will only truly have meaning if both the parent and the child are in agreement, so be sure to keep the lines of communication open about this issue.

A coming of age ritual is most often performed for girls when they have their first period (sometimes called a "first blood" rite) or for boys at around thirteen. There is often a version of "the talk," in which an adult or adults will talk to the child about what it means to be entering the realm of sexual activity.

Pagans do not have the same judgmental view of sexuality that many other religions share; sexuality is not considered to be sinful or immoral, nor is there a stigma against same-sex partners. During a coming of age ritual, there will likely be a frank discussion of the realities of sexual activity, with a strong emphasis on personal responsibility and informed choice.

Should you find yourself in the position of having this conversation during or prior to a coming of age ritual, presumably your child will have been raised with the usual Pagan values, and all you will have to do is remind him or her of the importance of those basic rules in the context of sexual activity:

- Harm none, which means never having sex if someone could be hurt by it (which may mean making the choice not to have sex with someone who is too young or inexperienced to make a considered decision on their own).

- The law of returns, in which you treat others the way you hope to be treated yourself, and remain aware that what you put out is what will come back to you.

- Personal responsibility and the rule of free will, which means that you are responsible for having safe sex and respecting the answer "no" if someone gives it to you.

- Words have power, so you must always be careful to speak with love and consideration.

- Magick is real and powerful—never misuse it to get sex or love from someone who is unwilling to give you those things freely.

- We are part of nature, and therefore it is natural for us to be sexually aware and interested, in whichever way that manifests. But we are also divine, and so we have the choice to rise above our animal nature until the time is right for everyone concerned. And when we do have sex, it is with a respect for the spark of the divine in everyone and with loving appreciation. Just because you can have sex doesn't mean that you should have sex. Be certain that you are honoring yourself and your partner with whatever actions you take and that love, on some level, is part of the equation.

Of course, a coming of age ritual isn't just about a child or teen becoming sexually aware/active. It is also about them taking the steps that begin to separate them from their parents and start them on the road to becoming their own person.

This can be a bittersweet moment for a parent. The ironic truth of parenting is that if you do your work well, you end up having to let go of what you value most. On the bright side, if you really did your job well, then you have not only raised an individual who will eventually take his or her place in the community and make valuable contributions, but you will also have forged bonds that will last long after the need for them is truly gone.

In many coming of age rituals, there is a ribbon that ties the teen to the parent or parents. The high priestess or high priest who is performing the ceremony (if one is doing so), or a relative such as a grandparent, will cut the tie that binds the child to the adults who raised him. This symbolizes the fact that the teen is now his own person, responsible for his own steps forward in the world.

Keep in mind that, depending on the age of the child, this is likely to be only a partial freedom in reality, and make that clear to the child before the ceremony so he doesn't have false expectations. Nevertheless, the point is that the child is now becoming an adult, and all those involved are aware of it.

Sometimes during a coming of age ceremony, adults from outside the family will step forward to demonstrate their willingness to act as a teacher, guide, or mentor for the child during his or her next stage in life. This is not instead of the parent but in addition to the adults who already contribute to the child's spiritual or practical education. A single mother, for instance, may ask a male friend to assist with the transitions that come with the teen years. Anyone involved should be aware of the responsibility and be willing to take on a long-term commitment for the sake of the child.

A child may wish to design her own ritual, have a parent write it, or rely on a community elder. As long as both parent and child agree, there is no right or wrong way to go about it. In *Circle Round: Raising Children in Goddess Traditions*, the authors have this to say about coming of age rituals:

The most successful rites of passage have several ingredients in common: meaningful participation and preparation by the child or adoles-
cent; community involvement; and recognition of the child's, adoles-
cent's, or adult's status by new responsibilities and privileges.

They then add a particularly helpful reminder:

Rites of passage should not be confused with initiation. Rites of passage recognize and facilitate the changes that come with maturation,
while initiation is a transformational ceremony of commitment to
Goddess tradition. Initiation can be taken on only by adults. (1)

This book is a valuable resource for anyone interested in coming of age rituals or any other issues concerning raising Pagan children, and I highly recommend that you take at least a quick peek before planning a ritual of your own.

Marriage

Marriage is one of the major rites of passage. It celebrates the joining of two
people in a bond that is at once spiritual and practical. It is no accident that
many people cry at weddings; there is little in life that is more moving than
watching two people take this great leap of faith together.

Pagan marriages can differ in some respects from the more conventional
sort usually seen in our society. For one thing, not all Witches choose to have
a legal wedding. Handfastings, the Pagan version of a wedding ritual, may be
either legally binding or not, depending on whether or not they are performed
by someone who is recognized by the state in which they are performed. (And
no, I'm not talking about a state of mind here.)

I became an ordained minister a number of years ago specifically for this
reason. My circle-sister Robin and her fiancé came to me and asked me if I
would be willing to take this step so that I would be able to marry them both
legally and spiritually. (Robin's husband is not a practicing Pagan, but he does
attend most of our sabbats and is very supportive of Robin's beliefs.)

I am not the only high priestess (or high priest) to become an ordained
minister so that she can perform marriages that are considered official in the
eyes of our society. I believe strongly that Pagans are entitled to the wedding

ceremony of their choice, and that they shouldn't have to choose between their religious beliefs and the law. The handfastings and weddings I've performed have given me some of the greatest joys I've experienced in my position as high priestess.

Of course, not all of the handfastings I've officiated at were also legal weddings. If you don't fill out the paperwork, a handfasting is just a handfasting, recognized by the gods and the members of our community but not by the world at large.

Sometimes this is by choice; some Witches choose a traditional "year and a day" handfasting rather than one that binds for life. Or they choose to not participate in a legal ceremony dictated by a society they feel does not represent their beliefs. Sometimes it is by necessity; my first wedding rite was for two women, and therefore there was no way to make it legal.

As Pagans, we don't differentiate between a legal ritual and a spiritual one. In the eyes of their friends and their community—and most importantly, in their own eyes—that handfasting was as serious a commitment as any accompanied by some official piece of paper.

Whether or not you choose to have a simple handfasting or a ritual that is a combination of Pagan traditions and those of a non-Pagan partner (as Robin did), there are certain elements that are likely to be a part of any Pagan marriage ritual:

THE RITUAL IS USUALLY HELD IN SOME SORT OF CIRCLE—For Robin's wedding, since most of those attending were non-Pagans, we put all the chairs in a circle (three rows deep, since there were over a hundred guests), and had the flower girl sprinkle rose petals around the outside to close the circle. Most of the guests had no idea we were creating sacred space, but it was a magickal circle nonetheless.

THE FOUR QUARTERS ARE CALLED AND THE GODS INVOKED—For a mixed ceremony, I recite a poem that calls on the aspects of the elements in a subtle way. For a strictly Pagan ceremony, you can simply call the quarters the way you usually do, although possibly in a more elaborate and formal manner.

THE COUPLE RECITES THEIR VOWS TO EACH OTHER—At this time, they will usually specify the length of the union, whether it is a year and a day, for as long as our love shall last, or 'til death do us part. Some couples have been known to say "through all our lives to come" with the intention of uniting in each incarnation that follows. Personally, I think that's putting a lot of pressure on a relationship, not to mention that vowing you will be together for all eternity is a little more commitment than anyone should be making, no matter how much they love each other right now. My advice, for what it's worth: take it one lifetime at a time. That's a big enough challenge for any marriage.

TYING THE COUPLE'S HANDS TOGETHER—Once the vows have been spoken, the officiant (the person performing the ceremony) will tie the couple's hands together with cord or ribbon, symbolizing that their lives are now bound together. This is an ancient tradition and the origin of the term "handfasting" (shortened from the older "hand-fastening") and the common expression "tying the knot." The cord is then removed and placed in a special box or pouch that the couple will keep someplace safe.

JUMPING THE BROOM—Another old tradition is for the couple to jump over a broom together, to symbolize the home that they will now share.

There are many variations on handfasting rituals, too many to go into here. Couples often light individual candles, then light a unity candle together and drink out of a chalice. There may be one officiant, a high priestess and a high priest, or even a Pagan and a non-Pagan minister. What makes a handfasting ceremony special is the intent of those taking part, not where or how it takes place. Love is our law and our greatest gift, and a handfasting ritual should celebrate that above all else.

No discussion of handfastings is complete without mentioning handparting rituals as well. It is an unfortunate fact of life that not all marriages or long-term commitments succeed. Even when both parties try their hardest, some relationships simply do not work out.

But as Witches, we realize that the vows made during a handfasting ritual go far beyond the legal or social level. The binding that takes part during a wedding that has taken place inside a sacred circle is a powerful piece of magick and affects those involved on a spiritual level as well.

For this reason, Pagans who are getting divorced often hold a handparting ritual to formally dissolve the connection they made earlier. If the parting is amicable, they may come together, preferably with the same person who offi-ciated at the original wedding and some of the original guests, and state their intention to unbind themselves from each other. If the couple is not comfort-able being in the same room, then each one can perform the ritual separately.

This ritual brings closure to the relationship emotionally, spiritually, and magickally, and it can help both partners to move on with their lives free of the ties they no longer desire.

Eldering

Although Paganism has been around since the dawn of time, Witchcraft as it is currently practiced by most of us is still a fairly young religion. We are only just starting to recognize the value of those who have been a major influence in forming and creating our spiritual path.

Eldering rituals are a way to celebrate the contributions of those who lead us. They can also be a personal celebration of the aging process—an open accep-tance of the next stage of a Witch's life, the counterpart of the more youthful coming of age. This is most often observed when a woman reaches menopause (in a ritual often called a "croning"), but men can also do eldering rituals at whatever age they feel is most appropriate.

An eldering is used primarily to mark the end of one stage of a Witch's life and the beginning of another. It may take place when a longtime group leader steps down from active practice and takes on the role of teacher or wise coun-sel instead. Or it may signify that a woman is no longer in the mothering phase of her life and is moving on to crone.

Pagans do not have the same negative attitude toward aging that burdens most of our society. Instead, we view growing older as a natural part of the cycle of life: birth, growth, death, and rebirth. We may not be thrilled with some of the changes that come with age, but we accept that they are the way of the universe and try our best to age gracefully. This doesn't mean that you can't dye your hair, should you so desire. But if you want to celebrate your gray hairs, there will be plenty of fellow Pagans willing to attend the party.

Passing Over

Like growing old, Pagans see dying as a natural part of life. This is not to say that we don't mourn the passing of those we love, but we do so because we will miss their presence in our lives, not because we think that death is something to be feared or hated.

Most Witches believe in some form of reincarnation, and we take comfort in the belief that we may someday be reunited with those who must leave us now. Many Witches also believe in the Summerland, a place of rest before the journey continues on to the next incarnation. The Summerland is said to be a place of eternal summer, warm and welcoming.

Death itself is just another part of the ongoing cycle, one that we will all take a turn at when it is our time. Many Pagans make plans for their own passing-over ceremonies, especially if they have enough warning to prepare. Friends may visit and be given last gifts, or old memories may be brought back into the light to be savored together one last time. Tears are just as likely to be from joy and laughter as they are from sorrow.

Pagan funeral rites can vary greatly. There is often a formal circle for invited guests, each of whom will share a story about the one who has passed over. There may be singing or drumming, or prayers for an easy journey to the Summerland. If the death was sudden and unexpected, those at the ritual may send light and love to help the deceased on their way.

Sometimes, especially if the death was expected and the passing-over relatively free of trauma, friends and family may skip the ritual and simply have a feast to celebrate the life of the one who has gone on.

It can be difficult for Witches who are in the broom closet if a loved one is given a non-Pagan burial because the rest of the family is of another religion or even just unaware of the wishes of the deceased. If you end up dealing with this situation, try to be considerate of the feelings of the other mourners. Attend the service if you can, and try to remember that all the gods are the same god, no matter what name is invoked during ritual. Afterward, you can have your own private Pagan memorial, and mourn in whichever way feels best to you.

If you are having a Pagan service, it is always nice to have a spell or prayer to recite together. Here is one that I wrote a few years ago; it was originally written for saying goodbye to a group member who moved away, but we realized that it could be used for more permanent goodbyes as well.

This spell can be said at the end of whatever ritual you are using, with no further embellishment. It is really more of a prayer than a conventional spell.

Spell for Saying Goodbye

We walked the sacred road as one
Brought together by fate and stars
Although our paths must part for now
In our hearts you're always ours
The circle stretches further now
The bond is bent but never broken
Our spirit still walks the way with you
Our love in all the words unspoken
Take our prayers and take our blessings
Journey safe and journey well
Know our thoughts will travel with you
And love will go to where you dwell
God and goddess hold you safe
And if they choose to grant our boon
Someday we will meet again
And dance beneath the Witch's moon (2)

Something to Think About:

If you are considering becoming an ordained minister in order to be able to legally perform handfastings or weddings, make sure that you are truly ready to take on this responsibility. Joining two people in marriage is a heavy obligation, one that requires you to be willing to take on part of the social and magickal weight of that union. It is not a task to be undertaken lightly. On the other hand, our community needs more people who are willing to take on this role, so if you are certain you are willing to make the commitment, by all means go ahead. Anyone can be ordained for free simply by going online and finding a site that does so. Be aware, however, that many of these sites are primarily Christian in origin and that some of them are clearly focused on money and not spirituality. (Some sites emphasis how much money you can make as an ordained minister rather than any spiritual benefits or obligations.) I don't advise getting ordained by any site whose philosophy or energy seems "off" in any way. The one I used, after much research and soul-searching, was Universal Ministries. Here is their statement of intent:

> The Universal Ministries is a nondenominational church founded in the truth of accepting the rights of all to follow their own personal beliefs without our intervention. We uphold the First Amendment of the Constitution of the United States of America, and the right of the individual to legally worship as they please. We uphold the Federal law that provides each church with the inalienable right to establish legal clergy and to appoint legal ministers within that establishment. (3)

Something to Try:

If you are going to officiate at Pagan weddings and handfastings, or if you want to write your own handfasting ritual, here are a few good books to use:

Magickal Weddings: Pagan Handfasting Traditions for Your Sacred Union by Joy Ferguson

A Romantic Guide to Handfasting: Rituals, Recipes & Lore by Anna Franklin

Handfasting and Wedding Rituals: Inviting Hera's Blessing by Raven Kaldera & Tannin Schwartzstein

Handfasted and Heartjoined: Rituals for Uniting a Couple's Hearts and Lives by Lady Maeve Rhea

Tying the Knot: A Gender-Neutral Guide to Handfastings or Weddings for Pagans and Goddess Worshippers by Jade River

And for women interesting in exploring their inner crone:

Goddesses in Older Women: Archetypes in Women Over Fifty (Becoming a Juicy Crone) by Jean Shinoda Bolen, MD

The Queen of Myself: Stepping into Sovereignty in Midlife by Donna Henes

Hidden Passages: Tales to Honor the Crones by Vila SpiderHawk

The Holy Book of Women's Mysteries by Z. Budapest

....

1   Starhawk, Diane Baker & Anne Hill, *Circle Round*, 322.
2   First published in *Llewellyn's 2008 Witches Companion*, 215.
3   From www.universalministries.com (accessed 20 February 2009).

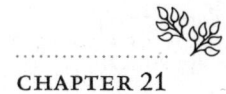

CHAPTER 21

Familiars

When a Pet Is Not Just a Pet

Pets fill many roles in our lives. They can be friends, companions, protectors, and foot-warmers. In addition to these weighty duties, some of them are familiars too.

In her book *The Enchanted Cat*, Ellen Dugan has this to say about cats:

> The cat's mythic role is that of familiar: a magickal companion and helper for the wise woman, cunning man, and, of course, the Witch. The links between the mystical powers of magicians and cats have been well established throughout time. Whether you realize it or not, a cat can serve as a cool, calm, and collected guide who helps us find and concentrate our own creative magick. They can and will assist us as we bring magick into reality by watching over us as a companion and a partner, lending their aura of wisdom and approving calm. (1)

Of course, a familiar doesn't have to be a cat, although felines tend to fill that position as often as not. Any animal that can form a close bond to its human can serve as a familiar, including dogs, rats, and any number of other critters. Some Witches even use snakes or lizards.

In the good-old, bad-old days, familiars were generally thought to be supernatural spirits, often in service to the devil, who aided Witches in their magickal work. Obviously, since Witches don't actually believe in the devil (strictly a Christian concept), we know this isn't true.

So what is a familiar?

My theory is that some animals are more sensitive to the energy generated by magickal work than others and also are more inclined to help in this area. (As opposed to helping you get rid of mice, trimming that annoying plant, or redecorating your furniture with those lovely gouge marks.)

For instance, I have five cats. Yes, I said five. Stop laughing. Anyway, they are all wonderful companions and bring me great happiness, but only one of them is what I would call my familiar.

Did I mention her name is Magic?

Let that be a lesson to you: be very, very careful when naming cats.

Magic the cat is clearly drawn to magickal work. When Blue Moon Circle gathers for a ritual in my living room, Magic invariably comes into the room as soon as we cast the circle. She strolls around the circle, greeting each member in turn—always walking deosil, mind you. Sometimes she stays under the altar table for the entire ritual, and sometimes she perches on a nearby couch and simply supervises from there.

If you leave the sage smudge stick unguarded on the table, she will jump up, grab it, and scatter it all over the floor—something she doesn't do with any other herb.

When I work magick on my own, she always comes over and stands by me, and she usually howls when I am reciting a spell. (I'm hoping that she is adding her feline energy to the rite and not just criticizing my word choice or syntax.)

She also co-authored my second book and often supervised my writing. Did I mention she's a bit bossy? But I truly believe that she adds a special something to my magickal endeavors, and that I would be a less powerful Witch without her.

That's what a familiar is.

I don't believe you can go looking for a familiar, no matter how much you might want one to aid in your magickal work. I think familiars come to you when and how they choose. (Especially if they're cats.) But if you don't have a familiar and want one, it can't hurt to ask the gods to send one your way. Just remember to keep your eyes and your heart open—maybe you already have one, and just didn't realize it.

Spell to Ask for a Familiar

For this ritual, you will want to put together a few items to represent the familiar you are seeking. For instance, if you want a feline familiar, you might have some catnip, a bowl of milk, or some cat treats, a piece of tiger's-eye, and a statue of Bast. If you are willing to let the gods send you whichever familiar suits you best, you can keep it more general; perhaps a special pillow or blanket that you will reserve for the animal and a bowl of fresh water.

You can also place a few of your magickal books and tools on a table, leaving an empty space to symbolize that you are making room for a new magickal companion.

After you cast your circle and call upon the appropriate god/dess (Bast is good for cats, for instance, or Hecate for dogs or snakes), spend a few moments in silence. Think about why you want a familiar and what you would offer the animal in return for its service.

Then open your heart to the possibilities, and recite the following spell:

> *Gods above, please hear my plea*
> *And send a furry friend to me*
> *One who knows and one who sees*
> *Magick and its mysteries*
> *To help me with my magick rite*
> *In light of day or dark of night*
> *To help me learn and help me grow*
> *To me a familiar now bestow*

Something to Think About:

Not all Witches want or need a familiar. If you are thinking about trying to get one, give some thought to what you want from a magickal companion. Do you just think it would be cool to have one, or are you really looking to add another element to your magickal practice?

Is it possible that you already have a familiar? If you have pets, feline or otherwise, think about how they react when you are practicing your Craft. Do they ignore you? Leave the room? Or do they seem drawn to the energy you are creating? If you aren't sure whether an animal is a familiar or not, do a ritual and watch carefully to see how your pet behaves. You may have to do this more than once to be absolutely sure.

....

1   Dugan, *The Enchanted Cat*, xxiii.

part six

the
natural
WITCH

The Importance of Maintaining a Connection to Mother Earth

For all the differences between various Witches and Pagans, there is one thing we all have in common, and that is a love and respect for nature.

Whether you are a Gardnerian who follows a traditional degree system or a Green Witch who practices on her own in the woods, you undoubtedly have an appreciation for Mother Earth and all the gifts she has given us.

Witchcraft is based in great part on a relationship to the natural world, with its cycles of change and its intertwining connections that bind us to each other and to all that surrounds us. Magickal work often draws on that link to the elements, the moon, and the sun, as well as to plants and other living creatures.

So what can we do to strengthen our ties to Mother Earth and best use her gifts? Can you still be a Witch if you live in the concrete jungle instead of the forest and rarely cast a circle outside?

Witches live everywhere and practice under very different conditions. The chapters in this section are aimed at helping you deepen your connection to nature, no matter what your circumstances might be, so that you can get the most out of your magickal work and your life as an Everyday Witch.

Something to Think About:

How do you connect to nature? Do you follow the moon cycles, plant a garden, or keep a pet? Is there one element that you are the most drawn to, such as water or earth, that helps you to maintain that tie? What can you do to strengthen your connection to Earth, our Mother—something you can add in to your schedule without too much trouble, so you will be sure to do it on a regular basis?

CHAPTER 22

The Witch's Garden

In days gone by, virtually all Witches had gardens. They grew the food that sustained them, the plants for their magickal work, medicinal herbs, and anything else that they might need. Of course, back then, almost everyone had a garden. A Witch might have grown more herbs and flowers chosen for their arcane properties rather than their beauty, but a garden was still a matter of necessity, no matter who you were.

In the modern world, that's all changed. Many Witches live in cities or apartments and have no place to plant a garden. Others choose not to have one for reasons such as a lack of time or a dislike of the chores that come with gardening. Some modern Witches don't have so much as a potted plant.

On the other hand, there are many of us who revel in our gardens, planting extensive and complicated plots of vegetables, herbs, flowers, and shrubs. Personally, I have a large garden for veggies, assorted fruit trees and bushes, a strawberry patch, an herb bed, and various flowers, shrubs, and trees. Some I grow to eat, some are decorative, and some, indeed, I use in my Craft.

So can you be a Witch without a garden?

Of course you can. Plenty of the Pagans I know don't grow more than the occasional spider plant, and they are just as spiritual and committed to their Craft as I am to mine.

Still, considering our connection to nature and the powerful boost a magickal herb can get from being nurtured by the one who will use it, I strongly suggest that anyone who can should grow some kind of Witch's garden.

A Witch's garden doesn't have to be as large as mine. A little patch of herbs by the front door will do—or even a small indoor garden if there is no place outside to put one. All you need is a windowsill, a few seeds, and a way to keep your cat from knocking the whole kit and caboodle onto the floor.

"Why go to all the trouble?" you might ask. Today's Witch can get herbs quite easily from the local health-food store without ever getting dirt under his or her nails, or order them from an online Pagan supplies site. Why take the time, energy, and bother to raise a garden of your own?

There are several reasons, actually. And you might want to give them some thought before you decide that a Witch's garden isn't for you.

Power and Intent

Many Witches use herbs, seeds, and other bits of plant matter in their magickal work (like a piece of apple wood for a wand or a section of tree for a Yule log). This is traditional, of course, and it also adds natural energy to our Craft workings.

And we know that much of the power of our magickal work comes from our focus and our intent, as well as our belief in our own abilities.

So think how much power will be added to each spell and ritual if the ingredients you use are permeated with that intent along every step of the process.

Suppose you were going to do some prosperity magick using basil, for instance. If you were growing the basil yourself, you could visualize your intent for prosperity as you sow the seeds, and again as you tend the plants, and again when you harvest them. By the time you finally use the dried herb in a ritual, it will be positively overflowing with potential energy for you to tap into as you say your spell.

And, of course, you could make pesto with the leftover plants, which isn't bad either.

If you do decide to grow a Witch's garden, you may want to figure out which herbs you would use most, and plant one or two of each. I am especially partial to herbs that have multiple purposes and can be used for magick, cooking, and sometimes even healing.

Therapy

If your reason for not having a garden is because your life is too hectic and there is no time or energy for such frivolous things, you are probably not alone. Most of us lead lives that consist of much hurried rushing from point A to point B and back again, with occasional stops to drop off the kids or pick up some groceries. We have become experts at multitasking, in order to squeeze every last drop of useable time out of the day.

Shockingly enough, this lifestyle has its downside.

For one thing, it's physically and emotionally stressful; you're likely to end up with high blood pressure and be short on sleep and out of sorts. What's more, it's not much fun. So much of your energy is spent getting from here to there that it is sometimes hard to remember why you undertook the journey in the first place.

Gardening is a simple, easy way to take a "time out." Even a few hours a week at a slower pace can help, and playing in the dirt is wonderful therapy. It can help you reconnect with your inner child and rediscover the elemental joy of watching things grow.

Depending on your needs, gardening can give you a few precious minutes by yourself or be an activity to share with your kids or significant other. Not only will you harvest herbs for your magickal work or clean, inexpensive vegetables for your table, you will be giving yourself permission to enjoy your own life again—and at a pace slower than the speed of sound.

Connecting with the Earth

Being a Witch is more than casting spells or looking good in black. At the core of our belief system is our connection with the gods and all living things. It is pretty hard to connect with nature if the closest you ever come is a day trip to a crowded beach or eating an apple that was trucked all the way across the country to get to you.

Don't get me wrong; I'm not saying don't eat apples. What I *am* saying is that if you want to make a real connection with the natural world around us, one of the best ways to do that is to have a Witch's garden.

If the only place you have ever gotten your food is from the grocery store, it is hard to really comprehend all that goes into that simple apple. If, on the other hand, you plant the tiny sapling, nurture it through rain and drought, fight off the bugs and the deer, wait three years, and finally eat that one perfect red fruit, you will have learned some valuable lessons.

You will have learned that the struggle to grow food is a lot tougher and more complicated than you thought. In addition, you may have gotten some insight into how hard our Pagan ancestors had to fight to survive, and why they thanked the gods for the rain and the sun and the fruit at the end of the harvest. You may have learned patience, too, and the joy that comes from reaping the rewards of your own hard work.

You may also have learned that you don't want to grow apples and want to stick with something easy, like lettuce. But that's a valuable lesson, too.

Can you learn all these lessons someplace else? Of course you can, and you probably will. But will you get an apple at the end, too?

Putting your hands in the dirt is the ultimate way to connect with the earth. (Although walking on a beach isn't a bad thing either, if you happen to have a beach.) If you scoop up a handful of soil in a healthy garden, you will see that there is much more to it than mere earth.

Most garden soil is a combination of clay and sand; getting the right balance matters. And if you look even closer, you will probably see that there is a thriving microcosm of life right there in your hands: worms, bugs, tiny critters you can't even see without a microscope. All of these small elements add up to a greater whole by working together. How's that for a lesson?

Our dependence on and interdependence with the living earth and all her inhabitants is of great importance right now, as all of that is jeopardized by humanity's greed and shortsightedness. Gardening is one way for us to make a personal connection with the natural world around us. And everything we grow gives back to the world in some small way.

For myself, I have also found that my Witch's garden is a conduit to connecting with the gods on a very intimate and personal level. When I am in the garden, surrounded by the sounds of the birds, the soft whisper of the wind, and the croaking of the toads in my woman-made pond, with dirt on my hands and my feet in the soil, I can feel the gods all around me. They are so present and so strong in all that's there, I sometimes think that if I turn around quickly enough, I will see the goddess on the other side of the garden, holding her own trowel and smiling at me with joy.

Nurturing a seed in even the smallest indoor pot is an act of power and of creation, and it connects us to the deity within and the greater natural world without. Even if you cannot have a big garden, I hope that you will try your hand at a small one, and see if you too can feel the goddess beaming over your shoulder when you do.

Something to Try:

Here are some of my favorite books on creating a Witch's garden and then making magickal use of all that you've grown in it:

Garden Witchery: Magick from the Ground Up by Ellen Dugan

Ellen Dugan is known as the Garden Witch, and for good reason. She is a Master Gardener with many years of nursery and garden experience, which she combines with many years of Witchcraft practice to create practical and inspiring books. Another good one by her is *Cottage Witchery: Natural Magick for Hearth and Home.*

The Wicca Garden: A Modern Witch's Book of Magickal and Enchanted Herbs and Plants by Gerina Dunwich

Bud, Blossom, & Leaf: The Magical Herb Gardener's Handbook by Dorothy Morrison

Country Witch/City Witch

Talking about gardens brings us to an interesting question: if you are a Witch, do you have to live in the country?

I can hear all you city Witches now, responding with a loud and resounding *no*! And, of course, you're right. You can be a Witch anywhere you want. It is a matter of belief and actions, after all, not of location.

But is it easier to be a Witch in the country, surrounded by nature?

Well, sometimes yes and sometimes no. (Helpful, aren't I?)

Actually, both have advantages, and each lifestyle is more a matter of choice and circumstance than it is a matter of "better or worse" or "right or wrong." The truth is, most of us live where we live for reasons that have little to do with our spiritual path.

Some of us live in a city because that is where our career takes us or because our partner prefers the urban life. Others live in the country because that's where we grew up and what we're comfortable with, or because we have chosen to move away from the noise and crowding to a quieter, rural setting.

It is certainly true that many Witches are drawn to the country, in part because of our love of nature and in part because being in the city can be tough on those with particularly strong psychic abilities (something that seems to be fairly common in the witchy population).

On the other hand, Witches are often gifted in the fields of art and creativity as well, and it can be easier to pursue a career in the artistic fields in a thriving metropolis.

There are certainly advantages to being a country Witch, such as being able to grow a big garden, walk in the woods, watch deer and geese and birds (and mice and skunks), raise animals if you want to, have a magickal circle in the back yard, and commune with nature on a daily basis.

On the other hand, there are some advantages to being a city Witch as well. It is almost certainly easier to find other Pagans, and you may have a choice of groups if you are interested in joining a coven. (In the country, you are often lucky to find even one.) There will probably be more Pagan bookstores and shops, and more large, open celebrations available to take part in, should you so desire. And bigger libraries, too.

And if you want to garden, most cities have community gardens that anyone can use. You don't have to tell people why you're growing that vervain, after all—they'll just think it's a pretty flower. Tee hee.

So live where you want and take the best of what that setting offers. You can always take trips to the country to visit the trees or travel to the city to attend Pagan events. Just make sure that wherever you live, you are making the most of your life as you walk the path of the Everyday Witch.

Something to Think About:

Whether you live in the city or the country (or somewhere in between), what are the aspects of your location that support your life as a Witch, and what about where you live makes being a Witch more difficult? Would you live somewhere else if you could?

Sacred Space Everywhere

There's a saying you've probably heard: wherever you go, there you are. It's true, actually. In the end, our magickal practice, herbs and athames, garb and spells, books and rituals all come down to one thing: us. As useful as all our tools are, they are nothing without those intangible qualities that we ourselves bring to the practice of Witchcraft: focus and intent, faith and strength of will.

Our beliefs in the tenets of Witchcraft—to harm none, the law of returns, personal responsibility and free will, the power of words, that magick is real and can create positive change, the connection with nature, and that the gods exist in all things—these are what make us truly powerful and truly blessed.

In the Craft, we say that there are five elements: earth, air, fire, water, and spirit. We are that fifth element, and that is the power we bring to each and every circle we cast.

When we work magick, we first create sacred space. If we work it well, we take a little piece of that sacred space with us everywhere we go. Being an Everyday Witch means that whether at work or at play, alone or in a crowd, we strive to keep that sense of the sacred alive in every moment of our daily life.

When you get right down to it, there is no line that separates our spiritual path from our everyday lives. If we truly walk our talk, these two things become inseparable, impossible to distinguish from each other. Our life is the journey to our spiritual goals, and sacred space is everywhere.

May it be so for you.

One Last Thing to Think About:
Stirring the Cauldron of Change

There is no growth without change nor progress without growth. We all have the power to use magick to create positive change in the world. Take a moment to think about what you do to create positive change—and in what ways you could be doing more.

How can you use your gifts to spread joy, help those who are in need, or make yourself a better person? What changes would you bring about with a wave of your magickal wand, if you had the power to do so?

Think about what's standing in the way of you making those changes, and make it your goal to remove those obstacles and manifest the change you wish to see in your life and in your world.

Live the life of the Everyday Witch with your every word, deed, and thought, and may the gods guide your steps on the path to beauty and joy.

Blessed be.

Resources and Recommended Reading

Ardinger, Barbara. *Pagan Every Day: Finding the Extraordinary in Our Ordinary Lives.* San Francisco: Red Wheel/Weiser, 2006.

Blake, Deborah. *Circle, Coven & Grove: A Year of Magickal Practice.* Woodbury, Minn.: Llewellyn, 2007.

———. *Everyday Witch A to Z: An Amusing, Inspiring & Informative Guide to the Wonderful World of Witchcraft.* Woodbury, Minn.: Lllewellyn, 2008.

Bolen, Jean Shinoda. *Goddesses in Older Women: Archetypes in Women Over Fifty.* New York: Harper Collins Publishers, 2001.

Budapest, Z. *The Holy Book of Women's Mysteries.* York Beach, Maine: Weiser, 2007.

———. *Summoning the Fates: A Guide to Destiny and Sacred Transformation.* Second edition. Woodbury, Minn.: Llewellyn, 2007.

Cole, Jennifer. *Ceremonies of the Seasons: Exploring and Celebrating Nature's Eternal Cycle.* London: Duncan Baird Publishers, 2007.

Cunningham, Scott. *Cunningham's Encyclopedia of Magical Herbs.* St. Paul: Llewellyn, 1985.

———. *Magical Herbalism: The Secret Craft of the Wise.* St. Paul: Llewellyn, 1982.

———. *Wicca: A Guide for the Solitary Practitioner.* St. Paul: Llewellyn, 1988.

Cunningham, Scott, and David Harrington. *The Magical Household: Empower Your Home with Love, Protection, Health, and Happiness.* St. Paul: Llewellyn, 1983.

Dugan, Ellen. *Cottage Witchery: Natural Magick for Hearth and Home.* St. Paul: Llewellyn, 2005.

———. *The Enchanted Cat: Feline Fascinations, Spells & Magick.* St. Paul: Llewellyn, 2006.

———. *Garden Witchery: Magick from the Ground Up.* St. Paul: Llewellyn, 2003.

Dumars, Denise. *Be Blessed: Daily Devotions for Busy Wiccans and Pagans.* Franklin Lakes: New Page Books, 2006.

Dunwich, Gerina. *The Wicca Garden: A Modern Witch's Book of Magickal and Enchanted Herbs and Plants.* New York: Citadel Press, 1996.

Emoto, Masuru. *The Hidden Messages in Water.* New York: Atria Books, 2004.

Ferguson, Joy. *Magickal Weddings: Pagan Handfasting Traditions for Your Sacred Union.* Toronto: ECW Press, 2001.

Fitch, Ed. *Magical Rites from the Crystal Well.* St. Paul: Llewellyn, 1984, 2000.

Franklin, Anna. *A Romantic Guide to Handfasting: Rituals, Recipes & Lore.* St. Paul: Llewellyn, 2004.

Galenorn, Yasmine. *Embracing the Moon: A Witch's Guide to Ritual, Spellcraft and Shadow Work.* St. Paul: Llewellyn, 1999.

Green, Marian. *A Witch Alone: Thirteen Moons to Master Natural Magic.* London: Thorsons, 1991.

Harrow, Judy. *Wicca Covens: How to Start and Organize Your Own.* New York: Kensington Publishing, 1999.

Henes, Donna. *The Queen of Myself: Stepping into Sovereignty in Midlife.* Brooklyn: Monarch Press, 2005.

Holland, Eileen. *The Wicca Handbook.* York Beach, Maine: Samuel Weiser, 2000.

Kaldera, Raven, and Tannin Schwartzstein. *Handfasting and Wedding Rituals: Inviting Hera's Blessing.* St. Paul: Llewellyn, 2003.

Kynes, Sandra. *A Year of Ritual: Sabbats & Esbats for Solitaries & Covens.* St. Paul: Llewellyn, 2004.

McCoy, Edain. *The Witch's Coven: Finding or Forming Your Own Circle.* St. Paul: Llewellyn, 1997.

Merriam-Webster's Collegiate Dictionary, eleventh edition. Springfield, Mass.: Merriam-Webster, 2003.

Morrison, Dorothy. *Bud, Blossom & Leaf: The Magical Herb Gardener's Handbook.* St. Paul: Llewellyn, 2004.

———. *Everyday Moon Magic: Spells & Rituals for Abundant Living.* St. Paul: Llewellyn, 2003.

O'Gaea, Ashleen. *The Family Wicca Book: The Craft for Parents & Children.* St. Paul: Llewellyn, 1992.

———. *Raising Witches: Teaching the Wiccan Faith to Children.* Franklin Lakes: New Page Books, 2002.

Penczak, Christopher. *The Mystic Foundation: Understanding & Exploring the Magical Universe.* St. Paul: Llewellyn, 2006.

Rhea, Lady Maeve. *Handfasted and Heartjoined: Rituals for Uniting a Couple's Hearts and Lives.* New York: Citadel Press, 2001.

River, Jade. *Tying the Knot: A Gender-Neutral Guide to Handfastings or Weddings for Pagans and Goddess Worshippers.* Cottage Grove, Wis.: Creatrix Resource Library LLC, 2004.

SpiderHawk, Vila. *Hidden Passages: Tales to Honor the Crones.* Niceville, Fla.: Spilled Candy Books, 2006.

Starhawk, Diane Baker, and Anne Hill. *Circle Round: Raising Children in Goddess Traditions.* New York: Bantam Books, 2000.

Sylvan, Dianne. *The Circle Within: Creating a Wiccan Spiritual Tradition.* St. Paul: Llewellyn, 2003.

Telesco, Patricia. *Your Book of Shadows: How to Write Your Own Magickal Spells.* New York: Citadel Press, 1999.

Trobe, Kala. *The Witch's Guide to Life.* St. Paul: Llewellyn, 2003.

Weil, Andrew. *Spontaneous Healing.* New York: Albert A. Knopf, 1995.

Weinstein, Marion. *Positive Magic: Occult Self-Help.* New York: Earth Magic Productions, Inc., 1994.

West, Kate. *The Real Witches' Year: Spells, Rituals and Meditations for Every Day of the Year.* London: Element, 2004.

Wood, Gail. *Rituals of the Dark Moon: 13 Lunar Rites for a Magical Path.* St. Paul: Llewellyn, 2001.

Worwood, Valerie Ann. *The Complete Book of Essential Oils & Aromatherapy.* San Rafael, Calif.: New World Library, 1991.